PRAISE FOR KEITH LOWELL JENSEN

"Hilarious. A demented masterpiece."

— *THE WASHINGTON POST* ON "ATHEIST
CHRISTMAS"

"You're gonna love Jensen's style of subtle, smart storytelling."

— *AUSTIN CHRONICLE*

"This book is a hilarious and ultimately a fair assessment of what it is like to be booked by the deep blue meanies."

— COMEDIAN, GREG PROOPS

T0022988

WHAT I WAS ARRESTED FOR

KEITH LOWELL JENSEN

CL◀SH

CONTENTS

INTRODUCTION BY GREG PROOPS

"The bullet that will kill me is not yet cast."

- Napoleon

"Quis custodiet ipsos custodes?"
"Who will guard the guards themselves."

-Juvenal The Satires

If you are smart, you'll have stolen this book and run arse over teakettle out of the store with the fuzz in hot pursuit. If you are wise, you will have bought this tome and be perusing it next to a crackling fire, sipping sherry. Chances are if you are white, you will never be arrested. I have been white most of my life and have experienced being stopped by the Arizona State Troopers, spun around harshly by a British Bobby given a nodding reprieve for smoking weed by bored SFPD in the 80s, and cursorily searched for weed by Jamaican Police whom I suspected of planting dope on tourists. But never arrested. This is where Mr. Jensen proves his mettle. The dazzling variety of arrests and exhaustive exotic locales for apprehension. Like Roseville, (a slumbering, sweltering, suburb of Sacramento), Seattle when

Grunge was the flannel monarch, Chicago which does suck in the winter, and Rocklin, hell knows where that burg is, speaks to his overarching need to face authority on its own terms and possibly an insidious criminal intent that he gives off like a fox emits pheromones. Police, for their part, can be nice, brutal, racist, unfeeling, brutal, kind, understanding, and utter Nazis. Sometimes all in an instant. Mr. Jensen has seen and felt it all. From the intrusive internal probes to the dehumanizing experience of bleeding profusely in front of an indifferent law enforcement physician. His scope and breadth of arrests will not only impress you with his willingness to dive deep into our haphazard and inequities justice system but also cast an illuminating light on what passes for police work in the land of the free. Read his tales with an eye toward the truth. There are good cops. There are also not good cops. This book is a hilarious and ultimately a fair assessment of what it's like to be booked by the deep blue meanies.

I GET ARRESTED A LOT

Well, I get arrested a lot for a white guy who doesn't drink. It's like saying a dog is old. You understand, it means they're old for a dog. They're old in dog years. I get arrested a lot in sober white guy years.

I don't trust people who haven't been arrested. How are you living your life? Take some risks, have some fun, live a little. Get arrested. Of course, if you're a brown-skinned person, gay, a woman, I understand why you don't want to get arrested, the stakes are higher. But my fellow, cis-gendered white dudes, come on! It's fun. And we're white dudes! It's not like we're gonna get in real trouble. And just think, while you're getting arrested, you're keeping some cops busy, cops that might otherwise be out harassing brown folks. It's a win/win. Use that privilege. Get yourself arrested.

Of course, an arrest record may not help when job searching. I have an advantage there. My arrests have made the job of stand-up comedian much easier. I keep these stories at the ready and I can always count on 'em when a set isn't going the way I want. No matter how distracted, drunk, or otherwise difficult an audience is, they will for some reason rally when I ask them if they'd like to hear about me being arrested.

Once, I was performing at The Crow's Nest, a notoriously rowdy room in Santa Cruz, California. After watching the opening and the middle comic struggle I pulled out the big guns straight away, and I scored with stories of cops, handcuffs, and drunk tanks.

Being a typical insecure stand-up comic, I fixated on the one person in the crowd who didn't seem to be having a great time. He sat with an angry look on his face through most of the first half of my set. I did a bit about my daughter teaching the Jehovah's Witnesses at our door all about dragons and at last, I had him cracking up. It was a crowd that really wanted crowd work, so I called him out, asking him what was up, why it was so hard to get him to laugh.

"I'm a cop," he answered, the smile I'd worked so hard for disappearing.

The audience gave an "Ooooooh" worthy of Jerry Springer. I spent the next ten minutes talking to him and the crowd loved it. He tells me about "Badge honeys," which is what they call cop groupies, and I tell him that people who like to have sex with comedians are called "Chuckle Fuckers" (and a horse with a horn on top of its head is called a unicorn).

The interaction with this cop officially moves me into killing it.

"I've got a story to tell that's better than any of your stories," he challenges. "If my story is better, will you buy me a drink?"

"How long of a story?" I ask, leery of relinquishing control of the mic and the stage.

He answers, "Five seconds."

"Five seconds!?" I reply. "Is that how long you think it'll take to punch my lights out?"

I finish my set, and I invite the cop onstage to give me his five seconds despite my better judgment.

He steps onto the stage, takes the mic, and tells me, "I'm not really a cop. I'm a nurse."

This brings the house down.

I buy him his drink.

A short while later the Coronavirus Pandemic shut down the comedy clubs. I'd not been away from the stage for more than a week in two decades and then suddenly I was at home on Friday nights, doing my best to entertain people who were also stuck at home as they watched me on their phones or laptop screens.

When I'm not Zooming, I'm writing. And it's not the same, but I like it. And hey, staying at home, I haven't been hassled by a cop all year.

PROTESTING WAR WITH HOUDINI

When I wore my first pair of handcuffs and got my first peek at the inside of a jail cell it was surprisingly consensual. I was 18-years-old, protesting the Gulf War, not the one we're still stuck in but its prequel, Gulf War I, Desert Shield. I imagine there's a guy out there who is proud that he named that war. Is there an equivalent to the gold record for people who name wars? A gold-plated depleted uranium bullet maybe? I'm no fan of wars, but Desert Shield, that's quality naming. Later wars with names like Operation Enduring Freedom, and Yippee, Let's Get That Fuckin' Oil, just don't have the same sparkle.

I went to see a doctor about a persistent cold as the tensions between the US and Iraq were building up. He asked me what I thought of the prospect of war, and when I told him I was against it, he pledged to keep me out of any military draft. A doctor had kept him out of Vietnam, he explained, and he was eager to pay it forward. I thanked him and promised myself then and there that I'd follow his example of going to medical school, and becoming a doctor, so I could help keep kids out of wars. Then I remembered that I couldn't even handle four years of high school, dropping out after year three, and I decided I'd just go protest the war instead.

I was at the protests around the clock as we headed toward the deadline that would surely result in an "exchange of hostilities." My boss at the time assured me my job was safe. She'd rather have been at the protests, she said, but she had a family to feed so she'd do her part by keeping our jobs safe if we chose to camp out on the west steps of the state Capitol building.

A few days into the protests, the old hippies who were experienced at protesting war explained that we were going to stage a 'die-in' at the nearby Federal Building, and we'd likely be arrested. They asked who would be okay with getting arrested and I stepped forward. On our way to the Federal Building, we'd march past the pro-war demonstrators.

My dad supported the war. He thought it was necessary. As a veteran himself though, he was offended by the rah-rah attitude being displayed by so many Americans.

I was proud to hear him say, "I think we need to do it, but I don't think we're supposed to fucking enjoy it. It's not a goddamn football game."

The yahoos who actually came out, using their free time to cheer on the bombing, to literally rally in favor of war, with big American flags, are the worse people ever and I hope that we can all agree not to ever, under any circumstances, have sex with them.

The night prior to the die-in, when things on both sides had quieted down, a heavyset man with shaggy hair walked away from the Capitol steps toward the street. Standing a few feet from the pro-war demonstration, he held up a boom box playing sounds of nuclear explosions.

A voice from across the street yelled, "Yeah! That's what we need to be hearing. Let's nuke the assholes!" to a chorus of cheers.

The next morning we walked silently from the Capitol to the Federal Building, passing the pro-war glee club on the way. We had lain down around the entrance. The cops, in front of the news cameras, explained that they'd be arresting us if we didn't disperse and gave us five minutes to leave if we didn't want to be. The cops, in front of the news cameras, started picking us up and carrying us inside. Two cops picked me up by my wrists and ankles and gently transported me into the building. Inside the building, there weren't any news cameras. They raised me as high as they could and dropped me. I landed on my back with a thud, and as I waited to regain the ability to breathe, they flipped me over and roughly put plastic zip-tie handcuffs on me.

They did not read me my rights and spoke to me only in short commands, "Get Up. Sit Down. Be Quiet."

We were all corralled into a big cafeteria-like room where we sat on the floor and got to know each other. One young man, with a stoic Buster Keaton-esque face did a mild little shimmy before standing up and walking to the nearest police officers who were seated at a desk trying to figure out how to process us all. Without saying a word he handed them the zip-tie handcuffs.

"Did you take these off?" a large, older cop asked.

The young man mimed the handcuffs falling off. The cops were not amused, but giggles sprang up around the room as the rest of us enjoyed the show.

"All right, turn around," the cop snapped impatiently before fitting our mute friend with a new pair of plastic zip-tie handcuffs.

He made a big show of pulling them extra tight. This pint-sized Houdini walked back to his spot on the floor, sat down in the awkward manner of one whose hands are cuffed behind their back, and immediately sprang right back up. Once again he walked to the cops at the desk and silently, without so much as a smirk, again brought his hands from behind his back and handed them their plastic zip-tie handcuffs.

Everyone not in a uniform broke out into fits of laughter and a few of the cops joined in in spite of themselves. Houdini mimed a "What? What'd I do?" mannerism at the now very angry cop who spun him around, and put four sets of plastic zip-tie handcuffs on him. The four pairs of plastic zip-tie handcuffs were then handed back to the cop with an even quicker turn-around than last time.

We cheered, we hooted, we hollered. The cops held every advantage and yet we were getting the best of them, at least for this fleeting moment. An escape artist mime wasn't going to stop the war or topple the power structure but at that moment it felt like a victory.

Red-faced, the officer stood up, found himself a pair of good old-fashioned metal handcuffs, angrily slapped them on Houdini's wrists, and pulled them tight enough to bring a small grimace to an up until now beautifully expression-less face. Our clown hero took a seat on the floor near me.

A middle-aged hippy whispered to him, "Can you get out of these ones?"

The still silent Houdini shook his head to indicate that he could not.

"It's cool, man. I have a key that should work."

We were instructed to stand up. As we marched out of the room to the holding cells, we'd pass the desk and the cops there would remove our cuffs.

I was behind Houdini when the big cop, perhaps feeling bad for getting angry earlier, said in a friendly voice, "All right buddy, let's get those off of you."

The entire experience was worthwhile if for no other reason than getting to see the angry, defeated look on that cop's glowing red face as Houdini casually handed him the metal cuffs and walked on by.

The mix of people in the cells was delightful; two cells of men, one of women, comprised of priests, nuns, hippies, punks, housewives, and Grandmothers For Peace. From teenagers to seniors we all laughed, traded stories, and talked about what to do next. A couple of hippies lit up a joint. A priest nearby asked them if this was a good idea, and they explained that they'd smoked pot in an impressive array of unusual places, but this was their first chance to cross 'jail cell' off their pot-smoking bucket list. The priest laughed, and I may have imagined it, but I swear he considered asking for a drag before thinking better of it.

A cop I hadn't seen earlier marched into the room and stood facing all three cells. Sounding like George C. Scott playing Patton, he addressed us. "While in this uniform my own political views are irrelevant and would be inappropriate to express, but what I can say is this; I'm proud of Americans such as yourself who are willing to stand up for their beliefs, even putting their own freedom and well-being at risk. Well done citizens."

And did he salute us? I remember him saluting us, but it seems so over the top that I'm forced to question my own recollection. I do know that he stood there as hippies, grandmas, priests, nuns, and punk rockers shook his hand, pat him on the back, and gave him their gratitude on their way out, not realizing that he'd largely taken the teeth out of our protest by bringing it to an uneventful, even cheerful finish.

On the trek back to the Capital we again passed the military intervention cheerleaders. They cleared a path for us to walk through, glaring at us with their arms crossed over their chests.

One of them said, "Keith? Keith Jensen?" and Lars, an old friend of mine from high school, stepped forward.

He was a big man in a camouflage jacket. I called him a moron. He called me a hippy. We had a hug and each went back to our side of the street.

WE'RE HERE, WE'RE QUEER , WE'RE FABULOUS, GET USED TO IT (DESPITE THE TITLE, THE LEAST FUN CHAPTER IN THIS BOOK)

Protesting the Gulf War gave me an unrealistically sunny idea of what protesting was like, and more specifically what dealing with the cops would be like. They were kind of brilliant during the war protests. We'd start a march, and they'd throw a parade permit at us and start blocking off streets for us. We'd change our route, they'd adjust. We had to head up onto the freeway before it became disruptive enough to actually register as a protest.

I remember thinking, "Wow they really learned some lessons from the 60s."

In the fall of 1991, California Governor Pete Wilson vetoed Assembly Bill 101 which would have given gays and lesbians protection from employment discrimination. I was on my way to the Natural Foods Co-operative market so I could make date night dinner for my vegan girlfriend when the protests just exploded all around me. Of course I joined in. What else would you expect from a guy on his way to the Natural Foods Co-operative market to buy vegan food?

My friend Kirk was with me and we were swept along, observing that the difference between this and the war protests was mostly just that this was a lot more fun.

There were drag queens and dancing and the chants

were great, "We're Here! We're queer! We're not going shopping!"

During The Gulf War protests some experienced protestors gave workshops on how to conduct yourself so that you didn't give the cops an excuse to crack your skull. Not that they wouldn't anyway, they explained, but your lawyer would be glad you followed this protocol when you fought the charges later. The instructions made sense: walk slowly, don't run. Your feet should never be more than a few inches off the ground. Keep your hands at your sides. Don't do anything that can be seen as a threatening motion. The boa twirling, whistle-blowing protesters dancing all around me hadn't received this same training it seemed.

There's a wonderful scene in the movie *Sid and Nancy* where the two title characters calmly walk through a riot. All around them is chaos with cops grabbing people, and their junkie calm leaves them virtually invisible as they glide through unscathed. This was me and Kirk as the protest made its way up the freeway onramp. I got separated from my friend as the cops grabbed glitter-covered party monsters and pissed off lesbians, but completely missed me moving slowly forward, not lifting my feet too high off the ground, keeping my arms at my sides.

Suddenly, I was alone, oddly, ominously, terrifyingly alone. I turned around and saw that after I'd slipped past them the riot cops had formed a line to hold the crowd back. They had their shields in front of them against the rest of the protesters. I was behind them. Behind them is not where shield-bearing riot cops want you to be.

A highway patrol cop on a motorcycle came rolling down the ramp from the freeway. He dismounted and rushed up to me. I turned to face him. He was just shy of 6 feet tall with thick, short grey hair, and a gray mustache on his pudgy face which was turning red as he screamed into my face.

"GET OFF THE OFF-RAMP!"

I turned 180 degrees and started walking back toward

the riot cops. I was walking even slower than before, not sure what I planned to do when I reached the line of cops.

Would I tap one of them on the shoulder and politely ask to pass? "Excuse me, I seem to have ended up on the wrong side here. If I could just squeeze through, everything will be right as rain again. Thank you."

Officer Motorcycle didn't like the speed at which I was following his orders and he gave me a nightclub enhanced shove.

"Run!" he yelled.

As I started to run, Officer Motorcycle ran after me. I veered to my right, to run off the side of the off-ramp but I didn't get very far before I was shoved to the ground. I thought I'd be arrested. I was ready to be arrested. Instead I was kicked in the face, hard.

This guy was nowhere near as cool as Ponch and Jon on CHiPs. I turned over on my back, to try and get up, and he straddled me, striking me in the face again. I was not fighting back.

With his considerable weight on my chest, I was struggling to breathe.

He looked me in the face and said, "You're going to die," and I believed him.

He wrapped his gloved hands around my throat and squeezed. I tried to get out from under him. The crowd had pushed the line of cops backward and the protest was now swallowing us. I struggled to get free, but I could not. Two cops pulled Officer Motorcycle off of me. I tasted blood in my mouth.

I looked to the side, and I saw Kirk yelling and being held back. I tried to run, to push into the crowd, but one of the cops who had pulled their maniac fellow officer off of me, had also managed to get a firm hold of my arm. She put me back on the ground, much more gently, and I was hand-cuffed. Another officer asked me my name, and I told her I wanted to remain silent. She said a reporter from the paper wanted to know my name and this felt like it might keep me safer. I told her my name and age, and that I was from Sacramento.

I was taken a few blocks to the main jail where every cop had been informed that I'd attacked one of their brothers in blue. I was screamed at and invited to try fighting now. Men twice my size, in uniforms, with guns on their hips, were daring me, begging me to take a swing at them. At 19-years-old I was a bean pole. That I was any kind of physical threat to these thugs was beyond hilarious. As they booked me I asked to see a doctor.

A woman claiming to be a medical professional of some kind took a quick glance at me and pronounced me, "Fine."

"Fine?" I asked. "My hair is plastered to my face with blood, and you haven't looked under it. I am not convinced that I'm fine."

She replied, "You can walk. And you can talk. You're fine," and with that, she left the room.

I had no ID on me. A cop with a clipboard asked me my name.

"Harvey Milk," I answered.

"Harvey Milk? The slain activist?"

"Damn. I didn't think you'd know him."

"Just tell me your name, idiot," he advised. I did.

"Are you gay?" he asked.

"You can't ask me that."

"I'm asking because if you're gay we'll give you a different colored jumpsuit, to help protect you from the other inmates."

"Is it pink?"

"What?"

"The special jumpsuit. Is it pink?" I was sure it was pink, even as I was prepared to be gobsmacked if it was pink.

"Yeah. It's pink," he answered, surely hearing the absurdity of his words.

I laughed out loud at this. "Yeah, that sounds real safe. Are you gonna ask me if I'm Jewish next? Got a nice yellow star for me?"

"Just answer the question. Are you gay?"

"No. I'm not gay," I answered

"Really? You're not gay." He looked up from his clipboard, his pen hovering.

He was going to double-check that he heard me right before putting this in writing.

"Really. Sorry to disappoint. Even if I was, I don't think I'd be into cops."

"Listen smart-ass, if you're not gay what were you doing out there?"

"Wow. I don't even know how to answer that."

Another cop fingerprinted me. I wasn't resisting him, but apparently, I'm not good at following instructions, even when I sincerely try. He screamed so much I felt like I was in a Monty Python skit.

"YOU DON'T MOVE YOUR HAND! I'LL MOVE YOUR HAND!"

I was having flashbacks to kindergarten when Miss Shepherd didn't trust me to make my own painted handprint on construction paper for my Thanksgiving hand turkey.

I've never felt so hated. I wanted to yell back at them. "I'm the one covered in blood! It's my own! That cop isn't the victim here!"

But for once I managed to keep my mouth shut. Finally, I got put in a cell, and so far I wore my own clothes, no special-colored jumpsuit.

The cell was crowded. I took a seat on a metal bench next to a Latinx man who looked to be in his early thirties and who did have a snazzy orange jumpsuit.

He looked at me, with my bloody face, and asked, "What are you in for?"

I laughed. It was just the classic question.

"Were you with those protesters blocking the freeway?" he followed up before I could reply to his question.

"Yeah…" I answered cautiously.

"You gonna save the world?" he asked, laughing.

"Gonna try, I guess. What are you in for?"

"Me, I'm here because they were transferring me to Folsom Prison, but you guys blocked the freeway so now I get to spend the night here. This is just a business trip for me, man. I make more money when I'm in than when I'm out," he said with a laugh.

His name was Jerry and we were swapping stories when two young white dudes were put in the cell. Apparently, they'd been arrested after getting into a fistfight with each other. Beavis and Butthead bee lined straight for me, maybe because I was the scrawniest guy in the cell other than them, maybe because I was already pre-beaten.

"Get up! We want to sit there!" Butthead snapped at me.

"Yeah!" Beavis added, brilliantly.

Jerry stood up and roared with way more power and authority than any of the cops had managed, "SIT ON YOUR SHOES! NOW!"

The two geniuses jumped to comply. First sitting down on the floor of the cell, then scrambled to get their shoes off their feet and under their butts. I was pretty sure Jerry didn't mean this literally but I couldn't blame them for not taking any chances. I wondered if, by jailhouse rules, this meant Jerry owned me now. If so, it was totally worth it.

Eventually Jerry went upstairs. The idiot twins soon followed. I was moved to another cell still on the ground floor. A lawyer named Sheryl came to see me. I was escorted to a special room where we talked through a thick plexiglass window. She explained that she was an activist and that she'd help me pro-bono. Then she explained to me what pro-bono meant. This was the first time I heard my charges and the news was not good. I was facing felony assault on a peace officer, peace officer being the hilarious part, and felony resisting arrest. I was no longer afraid that I was going to die at the hands of an enraged cop, but I was getting very scared that I had irreparably damaged my future, that I may be looking at actual prison time.

I remembered the child psychologist who once warned

my mom that Kids like Keith often ending up in serious trouble with the law.

I was returned to a crowded cell. Being stressed, bloody, and confined is a maddening combination. I felt like I was going crazy. I'd been beaten, threatened, screamed at, and was now potentially facing time in prison. I wanted to run, to go to my parents, to do something, but I was literally trapped, powerless, waiting to see what would happen to me next. It's an awful feeling.

The door to the cell opened and an officer with a clip-board stepped through it. "Okay, listen up; When I call out your name, step into the hallway, and face the wall. Undress, and bend over. Spread your cheeks apart and hold your balls out of the way."

He said this as casually as if he was giving a baseball team their positions. *All right, Tim, you got shortstop. Jeffrey, you cover 2nd base. Keith, spread your cheeks and get your balls out of the way.*

The names started and I stared in horror as men were humiliated.

If I wasn't mortified I'd have been incredibly amused at cops screaming, "GET THEM BALLS UP RIGHT NOW, GODDAMMIT."

Apparently spreading one's cheeks with one hand while holding one's balls up with the other is easier screamed than done.

I don't know that any man *wants* to take off their clothes and spread their cheeks while holding up their balls, though maybe it's a fetish I haven't come across yet, but I particularly did not want to do this. I am modest to an almost pathological degree. My closest friends have never seen my knees or even my ankles. When my daughter was three I realized I'd been avoiding taking her swimming because I didn't want to take my shirt off.

We were on vacation and the hotel had a pool. I decided it was time to address this body shame, modesty, whatever you want to call it, as it was now affecting not just my life but my daughter's as well. I walked her to the pool and at the last possible moment took my shirt off, picked her up, and prepared to hop in the water.

She looked at my chest, wide-eyed, and proclaimed loudly, "HA! Men have nipples!"

I got in the pool to the sounds of many laughs, feeling many eyes upon my nipples.

Yes. Yes men do have nipples, and they have balls and sometimes these balls must be kept out of the way. The names kept coming and the cell was emptying out. Officer Clipboard had surely heard about the wretched cop beater who'd gotten blood all over the innocent Officer Motorcycle's leather boots. Eventually, I was the only one left in the room. He smiled at me.

"One name left on my list," he announced and I started to stand. "Manuel Vasquez," he read, and I started to laugh.

"Ha! Oh man! I'm not Manuel. I'm Keith."

He yelled at me to show him my little plastic ID bracelet. I showed him my little plastic ID bracelet. He looked at his clipboard again, a sour expression on his face.

"I'll be back!" he announced, as he marched off and the door slammed shut behind him.

It was the first thing that had gone right since Jerry stood up for me against Beavis and Butthead. I felt joy and I grabbed a hold of it. I started drumming on the metal bench.

"Shut the fuck up, man," a voice demanded.

I looked under the bench, where a groggy-looking man was lying, staring back at me.

"Manny? Manny Vasquez? Dude! You just missed some brutal shit, man. They wanted you out in the hallway with your cheeks spread and your balls out of the way!" Manny turned over and went back to sleep.

"I'll be back" turned out to be an empty promise and in the morning my friend Chris and his mom, a minister, came to pick me up.

Her church had put together the money for my bail.

They took me to see an actual doctor. My wrists were bruised up, and I had cuts on my forehead but nothing was broken and they didn't think I'd suffered a concussion. I wanted to go to sleep. I was so excited at the thought of my own bed. But first I wanted to have a nut burger from Greta's Cafe.

Someone at the cafe sarcastically complimented me on, "Making a gay rights protest all about me."

I didn't have the energy to reassure them that they were right, that I had gotten beaten up and charged with two felonies on purpose, for the attention. I took my nut burger and headed for home.

"Keith, this is mom. Are you in jail? Call me."

"It's dad. Call."

"Where are you? Call us."

My answering machine was full of message after message from my parents. I dialed their number.

"Is there something you need to tell us?" my mom asked.

"Yeah. I got arrested last night."

"Yes, we know. Is there something else?"

"What?" I asked, perplexed.

I was too tired for this. I just wanted to eat my food and go to sleep in my bed, my wonderful comfy bed. Apparently The Sacramento Bee had mentioned that there was one arrest at the local protests, "Keith Jensen, Gay, of San Francisco." Nice for my name to be the only detail they got right.

"Yes, mom. I was arrested. No, I'm still not gay. Quit asking. And I haven't been secretly living in San Francisco either. I need to sleep. I'll call you later."

My dad and I met with Sheryl, the lawyer who'd come to see me in jail. She showed us the police report which was verifiably untrue on many counts including a claim by Officer Motorcycle that there were glass bottles being thrown at him. Multiple eyewitness accounts including from journalists and from other cops failed to mention any bottle throwing. It looked likely, she explained, that they'd reduce my charges to misdemeanors and that I'd get credit for time served and not have to do any additional jail time. This was a huge relief. I was told that I'd even be able to have it expunged from my record eventually.

The charges are still on my record. I have not had it expunged. It feels wrong somehow, the way some people feel about having a tattoo removed. Yeah, that skull on your chest with a peace symbol and an anarchy "A" for eyes was probably a bad idea, but it's a part of your history, of who you are. So both charges remain on my record but I have no tattoos.

I asked Sheryl if we could sue their asses off, and told her I had countless witnesses and photographs. She thought there was a good chance we could.

A week later I couldn't get in touch with her. She disappeared. The law office where she worked informed me they had no forwarding information for her and that she had been handling my case on her own, outside of her employment with them. I try not to buy into conspiracy theories but... what the hell, let's go deeper, shall we?

Officer Motorcycle was suddenly sitting on his motorcycle every morning on a corner two blocks from my house. There was no reason for a highway patrol officer to be stationed there, on a not particularly busy corner in an area that was not anywhere near a highway onramp.

He'd say, "Good morning," to me with a smirk as I passed him on my way to work and as soon as I was a block past him, he'd start up his bike and leave.

The lawyer disappearing and the cop suddenly greeting me every morning was terrifying, and it made me feel paranoid, made me question my own sanity. I wanted my life back and it felt like it was trying to come back, like it was there waiting for me, the normal loves, disappointments, adventures, frustrations, and broken hearts. I didn't want my life to be about this one night, maybe the worst night of my life. I wanted desperately to move on, even as I also wanted some sense of justice.

At the time I was working at a coffee shop called Coffee, Tea, and Company that rented space inside the Natural Foods Co-op.

Two cops came in and as they reached the front of the line I said, "I'm sorry. I don't serve pigs," and I went to the back to do some dishes.

My co-worker Craig rushed back from his break to take their order. They sat in the dining room and glared at me, but they didn't say anything, or harass me, or even complain to the manager. I think I needed to feel like I didn't have to be afraid of them. To experience that I could interact with cops, interact with them negatively even, and not have my life and freedom threatened. I had lived with the privilege that comes with being a white dude all my life, and I was desperate to confirm that it was still there. It was.

I never heard from the lawyer again. After a week I stopped seeing Officer Motorcycle on the corner.

I moved on with my life. That cop probably had a nice retirement, but maybe, just maybe, there's justice in the universe and he choked on a cruller and died.

THE GUITAR LESSON

I was sixteen hanging out with my friends Bill and Ryan at this older dude, Andy's apartment, and Andy was trippin' hard on acid.

Andy was a heavy-set, short Mexican man with beautiful long black hair that he wore in a braid reaching down to his belt. His ratty old apartment was a favorite place to hang out, with a large television and an amazing stereo system, supporting an impressive library of records and movies on videotape. And occasionally he'd get out of his head on acid and things would get interesting.

Andy went downstairs to talk to his neighbor, and he comes back noisily, disheveled and sweaty screamin' how he's gonna stab a dude. He runs back out the door after grabbing a big old kitchen knife, Billy running after to try and stop him from committing a murder.

Ryan and I are hella freaked out, frozen in place, and more so when we hear multiple police sirens growing closer. Andy's old hippy roommate, whom we don't really know, comes out of his bedroom in jeans and a Pink Floyd concert t-shirt with the sleeves cut off, his feet bare.

In an authoritative voice he snaps at Ryan and me, "Come with me into my room, now."

So of course us two teenagers follow this adult stranger

into his bedroom. He shuts the door, hands us each a guitar. He sits down with his own guitar and starts playing, and singing.

His song went something like this:

"We don't know nothing about that noise out there. We're just having a guitar lesson

I just rent a room here, and you are my students. Oooooh, we sure hope everything is okay."

The bedroom door opened and a cop peeked in.

We all looked up at the cop, and the hippy said, "Can I help you, officer?"

"What's going on in here?"

"I am a guitar teacher and these are my students. We heard yelling. Is everything okay out there?"

"Is this your apartment?"

"No, I just rent a room."

"...okay." The cop shut the door, and the hippy started giving us a guitar lesson in earnest.

Man, I love that hippy.

CHICAGO O'HARE

Following my beatdown by the cop at the gay rights protest, I dealt with a hard breakup and a partial make-up, and a sense of youth being squandered. It all added up to me feeling like I really needed to get out of Sacramento.

Enter Spike and Mike's Festival of Animation. I've loved this show since I was a kid in a suburb of Riverside, California and my dad took me to UC Riverside to see it. Now they'd come to Sacramento and I learned that they traveled to college towns all over the country with a road crew who'd distribute flyers, man the merch tables, and drink and do drugs. It was like the circus had come to town and I'd be damned if they'd be moving on to the next town without one more clown.

I insisted they hire me, literally. I quit both of my jobs and started showing up for work with the rest of the flyer crew. After three days in a row of this I'd worn them down, and finally, Mike came to agree with me that I did indeed work for him now, whether he liked it or not.

From Sacramento, the show would be heading to San Francisco after a quick dip down to San Diego to pick up flyers and to give Spike a chance to meet this kid who had strong-armed Mike into hiring him. Spike, I discovered, had me scheduled to go to Texas but when I walked into the office with my head shaved save for my long blonde bangs which I had braided, a different color of rubber band at the end of each braid, he decided he'd better switch me to the San Francisco crew.

San Francisco begat San Jose, San Jose begat Riverside, Riverside begat Newport, until eventually, I ended up in Chicago far away from the cops who'd beaten me up, and the girl who'd broken my heart.

I hated Chicago. The fun part of this job was meeting people in a new town each month. In Chicago, I met a girl who stood me up, twice! Fool me once, shame on me. Fool me twice, fuck you Chicago.

The crew leader in this town was a very macho dude named Matt Sharp. He'd managed to get his friend, Nick, hired so they mostly hung out with each other and left us alone, with no car. And also, it was freezing. I showed up in Chicago with no jacket. I knew it would be colder than Southern California but I wasn't ready for this icy wind that made my bones ache. Even though I had no rent to pay, no monthly bills at all, I still managed to be broke most of the time. I had to deal with the freezing Chicago spring for a week, until I got paid and could run to the big thrift store to buy the cool corduroy jacket I'd spotted in their window the first day we got to town.

I was cozy and warm in my cool new used corduroy jacket as I made the rounds pushing flyers into hands at the college bars when a dude handed me a dollar, followed by another dude handing me a dollar, until finally I asked the third dude who handed me a dollar why people kept handing me money.

"Aren't you out here asking for money?" he asked, perplexed.

"What? No. I'm out here passing out flyers for Spike and Mike's Festival of Animation."

"Well that can't pay much," he snapped back, defensively.

"They pay me pretty well, and rent me an apartment in town. They flew me here from California."

"Well then why are you dressed like that?"

"Excuse me?"

"Why are you wearing that jacket?" he asked, taking back his dollar and not waiting for my answer.

I hate Chicago.

I should have been having a blast. I was there with my best friend Dan, whom I'd recently convinced Spike and Mike to hire. But we mostly just drank, got thoroughly sick of each other's company, and failed to find the cool kids to show us the fun side of Chicago. Dan woke me up one morning with the news that the USSR was collapsing.

It was a surreal feeling, watching the tanks roll through the streets of Moscow, and then getting up and going about our lives as if the Cold War enemy our country had been in a tense, potentially apocalyptic standoff with for as long as we'd been alive was just... suddenly... gone.

Dan needed some dental work and he pretended to be non-verbal at the dentist's office so that I could go in with him. I had front row seats as his wisdom teeth were removed. The doctor jokingly offered to let me pull one of 'em out. I'd normally say a funny dentist is a terrible thing, but it's not so bad when you're not the one in the chair. By the time we left Dan actually was nonverbal, his mouth packed with gauze, and blood which he had to spit out frequently.

Rather than go home and rest, we enjoyed the unplanned day off by going to the Art Institute of Chicago to check out the Magritte exhibit. Sitting on the steps in the sunshine afterward, we forgot for a minute that we hated Chicago. We discussed the exhibit, Dan writing notes on a small pad, and we noticed a cute woman watching us.

Dan scribbled, "This is perfect. I'll go say hi! Being able to write instead of talking I'll be confident for once!"

I encouraged him, as she was definitely flashing some flirty smiles his way, and I realized he did look pretty adorable in a tragic hero sort of way, with his Ray-Ban framed glasses, and his mess of curly, partially dreaded red hair, writing notes to his friend on the steps of an art museum.

He scribbled, "I'm gonna go talk to her. Wish me luck."

"Good luck," I told him, as she turned her full attention to us, just waiting for him to approach.

In preparation, he spat a mouthful of blood out on the white steps. I watched her smile turn to disgust. She grabbed her small pile of books and rushed down the steps, away from us. Dan sat back down.

"Dude," was all I could say, all there was to be said.

Of all the Dans in the world, he was the Charlie Browniest.

Finally, the day came for us to make our escape. We wrapped the show and went out for drinks with Matt and Nick. We'd fly to San Diego in the morning, I'd attend my grandparents' 50th wedding anniversary, and immediately afterward rush to board another plane, this time flying to Seattle, where Spike and Mike were better established. With Nirvana blowing up, Seattle was the current IT city for youth culture which seems a bit cheesy looking back but truth be told, the hype was working and I was excited not only to get the hell out of Chicago but to see what Seattle had to offer.

Come morning Matt and Nick decided there was time for a few games of pool at their favorite bar. One flirty bartender and too many morning beers later we realized we had lost track of time.

"Oh shit, we gotta go!" Matt commanded suddenly, hanging up his pool cue and racing for the rental cars.

We'd likely still make our flight, but it was gonna be tight. I was in one rental car with Matt, and Dan was in the other with Nick. As we got to "Departures," Matt told me to grab our bags and head to the gate. He'd return the rental car and meet me there.

You know the announcement at the airport that tells you

never to take anyone else's bag? Yeah, that, it turns out, is really good advice.

I ran to the security checkpoint. Luckily this was before the September 11th terrorist attacks, and so getting through security didn't take as long. I threw my big backpack and Matt's gym bag on the conveyor belt. The woman working the x-ray machine got off her stool.

"Is this your bag?" she asked, pointing at Matt's oversized Adidas duffle bag.

"Sort of," I answered.

"There's something in it that looks like a gun."

"Oh. Well… we're entertainers. I'm sure it's a prop."

"I have to call someone over to search the bag."

Again, this was pre-September 11th, so they didn't have as many people manning the security checkpoints. "I'm sorry, I'm about to miss my plane. Can I just open the bag, and we can take out the toy gun, or water gun, or whatever it is and toss it?"

"No. I'm sorry. You're not allowed to open it either."

"Okay. I'm gonna run to the gate and see if my boss is there yet. It's his bag."

"You can't leave."

I left.

"I'll be right back," I called behind me as I hurried off toward the gate. I didn't find Matt and was hurrying back to security when suddenly I noticed a man in a suit walking next to me, keeping pace. I sped up, he sped up. I slowed down, he slowed down.

"Hey man, can I help you?" I asked, slightly annoyed.

"You Sharp?" he asked.

Now, I was used to Sacramento cops asking us if we were SHARPS meaning Skinheads Against Racial Prejudice. Cops couldn't tell the difference between a skinhead and any other punk. If they saw boots, they saw a skinhead, and unfortunately, it is my experience that cops are more concerned with the anti-racists than with those the anti-racists are fighting. With these experiences in my recent past, I responded to the dude the way I usually responded to this question in Sacramento. I showed him my long hair, hanging in my face, bleached almost white.

"Do I look like a SHARP?"

"Matt Sharp?"

"Oh, Matt! No, I'm not Matt Sharp, but I am the dude with Matt Sharp's bag."

Next thing I know I'm face down on the ground with a knee in my back, my arms wrenched behind me. There is shouting and hectic movement all around me. More people in suits and some officers in uniform have shown up. They get me to my feet and things are real tense. I start to get nervous, giggling nervous.

"Hey, I'm not fighting. This is just a misunderstanding, and I'm cooperating." To my amazement, this works and they handle me more gently and everyone is a small degree calmer.

The guy in the suit walks me to the x-ray machine that I'd skipped away from moments earlier.

"Yeah, that's him," the woman at the machine IDs me.

I see a table with Matt's bag on it, and Matt's gun, a black, metal, and very much real gun.

A cop in uniform is in my face. "You're in trouble. You're in a lot of trouble. You're going down."

Not knowing what the proper response to 'You're going down' is, I try spilling my guts. "The bag and the gun belong to…"

"Oh no, no, no, no," she interrupts me. "You're not putting this off on anyone else. You had the gun. You're going to jail. You're busted."

She's really excited.

"Okay, but I'm not alone…" I try again.

"You're the one here in handcuffs, buddy. You're the one who is going down for this."

"Look, don't you wanna bust the whole gang? I'm going down, but I'm willing to sing! I'll rat out the whole lot of 'em!" I plea, desperately, figuring I might get somewhere if I matched her old-timey crime noir patter.

Finally, another cop came over and suggested she go do something somewhere else.

"Who is Matt Sharp?" they asked me.

"He's my boss. I'm sure he just forgot it was in there. We were late for our flight." I let them know what gate Matt would be at, and a few minutes later I see Matt, handcuffed, being escorted toward me by two more cops.

"Dude, I am so sorry," Matt said as soon as he was within earshot. "I forgot it was there."

"I'll need time and a half for this," I replied.

I was pretty sure I was out of trouble now, or at least on my way to being out of trouble, but I wondered how long this would take to be cleared up. After much frantic activity by an army of cops in uniform and in plain clothes, we were taken to holding cells in the airport.

Matt and I shared a cell. Next to us were two guys who'd been arrested having sex in a stolen truck in the airport parking lot and who were now being subjected to Chicago cops crackin' homophobic jokes. Personally, I was impressed by that level of passion. I don't think I've ever been so turned on by anyone that I'd be willing to go for it in an airport parking lot in the middle of grand theft auto. I mean, I love my wife but when we're stealing trucks at the airport, she can just wait. Sadly, I can't imagine things went well for them.

Matt finally had an opportunity to try to explain to me why he had a loaded pistol in his luggage. It seems the bosses gave him a budget to hire a security guard to walk the evening's receipts to the bank each night. Matt brought his gun with him, walked the money to the bank himself, and kept that security guard money. He says he meant to check the gun when he got to the airport. I didn't believe him. He shoved it deep in one of his boots, and I think he meant to try to sneak it through, just as I'm pretty sure he'd done on our flight to

Chicago. He says he didn't remember it was in there when he had me carry his luggage. On this point, I do believe him. I knew him pretty well by this time, and he was a good dude.

From the airport jail, we were loaded into a van. Rather than seats, they had an odd setup wherein our backs were against a corrugated steel wall bent to allow us to bend our knees slightly. We were halfway between sitting and standing, and it was less comfortable than either. Bars like those on a roller coaster came down to hold us in place, and this was appropriate because the driver was a maniac. I didn't have a great view, but I swear at one point we took a private cop-only road that went across a freeway sideways. I kept seeing the action movie scene in my head where we get hit by a truck and the cops die, but Matt and I survive, only to have to go on the lam, blamed for the cops' deaths that we had nothing to do with. I'd like to have Joan Cusack play me in the movie, please. I love her.

We arrived at what I assume was the main jail but we were kept on our own, just the two of us in a cell.

I kept asking Matt, "What are you in for?" and he kept telling me to, "Shut up."

They took my belt and shoelaces away, and I was wearing big raver pants so the belt was sorely missed. I pulled some threads from the deteriorating lining of my corduroy coat and tied my belt loops together. My pants now stayed up fine, and it's kind of ridiculous how proud I was of this bit of ingenuity. Yeah, bring the apocalypse, I'm ready! I don't know about the rest of you, but MY pants'll be staying up!

Matt sang "Sitting on the dock of a bay" repeatedly; not the song, just that line, over and over and over again. Apparently that was the only part of the song he knew, and yet he felt that was sufficient for him to belt it out at top volume. I was relieved when the guards interrupted him to offer us food. Bologna sandwiches on white bread. I asked if they had a vegan option, less because I thought they'd actually have a vegan option than that I thought it would be funny to ask if they had a vegan option. They did not have a vegan option. I took a bologna sandwich, and I gave it to Matt.

"If we end up in prison, you owe me a pack of smokes for that," I told him.

I was promised I'd be out in an hour since Matt admitted the gun was his. They just needed to check my record for warrants and they'd process me and get me on my way.

Thirty minutes later they asked me if I'd ever heard of "The Revolutionary Communist Youth Brigade."

I laughed, realizing I'd not be getting out of jail as quickly as I'd hoped. I had indeed heard of The Revolutionary Communist Youth Brigade. I'd let a bunch of them crash at my place the previous year when they came up to Sacramento from LA for a May Day event.

The police listing people as communists would of course be frowned upon in this day and age, but there is a Gang Task Force, and labeling the RCYB as a gang allows them to list a person as a member of said gang, which is essentially listing this person as a communist and the affiliation was enough to cause me to have to spend the night in jail in Chicago. Funny thing is, I'd spent my night with the Revolutionary Communist Youth Brigade drinking their beer and debating with them about the merits of capitalism. I didn't convert any, but damn it America, I gave it my best shot! Every time we stepped outside my apartment for a smoke we'd see the cop car circling the block. It felt very 1950s. On the off chance that any of the comrades are reading this, I'm still not a communist but hey, you were more right than I was. Capitalism is trash.

Matt used his one phone call to call his lawyer. I wondered if I'd ever be able to use the phrase "My lawyer."

Having a lawyer, whose phone number you kept handy, seemed like a level of adulthood I'd never reach.

I used to call my friend Brett on speaker phone and when he answered I'd yell "Wilson."

This was his cue to pretend he was a lawyer.

I'd tell him what my problem was, "I got this guy here

says he's charging me full price for a coffee refill!" and Brett would yell, "WHAT?! FULL PRICE! TELL HIM WE'LL SEE HIM IN COURT! WE'RE GONNA NAIL HIS BALLS TO THE WALL!"

That was his favorite phrase, he was all in for nailing balls to walls, he was from the old balls to walls school of law. He'd go on to cite precedence, making up cases.

"MAYBE HE'S NEVER HEARD OF JONES VS. DUTCH BROTHERS? THIS IS AN OPEN SHUT

THE UGLY STICKS VS THE NIGHT STICKS

I was in a band called The Ugly Sticks. We were pretty good, but our name was great. Our friend Rob Cockerham, of Cockeyed.com fame, threw a Cinco de Oktoberfest party because the fifth of October fell on a Saturday and that's reason enough.

The theme was an offensive and hilarious mashup of Mexican and German culture. A Jell-o mold in the green, red, and white of the Mexican flag, with sauerkraut strands and bratwurst encased in it, and worst of all, someone made or managed to procure a swastika pinata. Why are pinatas usually shaped like donkeys, Batman, and Sponge Bob? I like them guys. Beating the shit out of a swastika would be way more satisfying. Hopefully, it'd be full of German candy. Sorry Mexicans, you win when it comes to food, but on candy, the Germans got you beat, and honestly, their candy isn't even that good.

The Ugly Sticks would provide the musical entertainment. We didn't have a klezmer/mariachi theme or anything, we were just gonna do our usual 60s garage rock-influenced set. We had no plans to acknowledge the party's theme at all, until the cops showed up that is.

Cops often showed up when we played. Look, let your neighbors make some noise on Friday and Saturday nights,

ya scrooges! Who the hell calls the cops on a band playing a
set that's under 60 minutes long before 10 p.m. at night?
Usually, the cops would tell us to wrap it up. We'd tell them
we had two more songs. They'd say okay. We'd play four
more songs. And we'd wrap it up. Sometimes the cops
would even hang out and enjoy the music.

On this occasion they marched right into the backyard
and told us to stop playing.

"We only have two more songs," I offered to the nearest
cop.

"No. You don't," the cop answered back.

At this point my mouth took over, without checking in
with my brain first. This is not an uncommon occurrence.

I listened, helplessly as my own voice came through the
speakers announcing, "Okay, that's our set for the night. I'd
like to thank the Sac PD for sticking with this evening's
theme and acting like a bunch of fucking Nazis."

We went about breaking down our equipment under the
hateful gaze of two cops, then four cops. I picked up my PA
head and headed to my van, now six cops. A cop came at me
from the alley.

"Drop that," he ordered.

"Drop my PA? Why?"

"I said drop it."

"No. It'll break. I'll set it back in the backyard and then
you can arrest me or whatever."

"You'll drop it right now! That is an order!" he barked,
putting his hand on his gun.

My little brother came over and took the big bulky piece
of equipment from me. The cop grabbed me by the arm and
put me against the back of his car. With my hands on the
trunk, he kicked my feet apart, the whole badass cop move
that he probably first fell in love with while watching
Starsky and Hutch or CHiPs on TV as a kid.

He handcuffed me, doing the old extra tight handcuffs
trick, and put me in the back seat. I sat there for a minute,
wondering how far down the rabbit hole I'd go this time.

With all my trips to jail, I'd managed never to get sent upstairs. Despite that I'd done nothing wrong, I wondered if this would be the time. I had a record, and the cop was really angry.

As I sat in the squad car wondering what I'd just set in motion, another couple of squad cars pulled up. One of the new cops on the scene, a black man in his forties, was clearly in charge. The other cops came to fill him in on what happened and you could see that he commanded respect.

He looked at me, and asked the cop who'd put me in the car, "What did he do? Why is he in the car?"

"He called us Nazis," the younger cop answered, clearly expecting a reaction.

The older cop just looked tired. "He called you a Nazi?"

"He called us all Nazis. He said cops were Nazis," he said, again with a voice that seemed to ask, "Can you believe it?!"

"He's allowed to call us Nazis. Get him out of the car."

"What?"

With a sigh, he repeated himself. "He's allowed to call us Nazis. Get him out of there, now."

The younger man was frozen with frustration, "Well… can we take him for a ride first?"

"No, you can't take him for a ride," the older cop answered, shaking his head and sounding exasperated. "Get him out of the car, now!"

I don't know for certain what he meant by "for a ride" but I'm pretty sure we all know what he meant by "for a ride" and, well, I'm glad I didn't go "for a ride."

MARSHMALLOWS

I was 16-years-old when I was caught shoplifting marshmallows from the Bel Air supermarket on Cirby Way in Roseville, California.

I looked cool.

I had on a leather jacket I'd inherited from my Grandpa Eddy. He was a slight man and the jacket was a couple of sizes too small for my tall lanky frame. This awkward fit was exactly what I loved about it as I thought it made me look like one of The Ramones, a blonde Ramone, with acne. As cool as it made me feel, it was far from the best choice for shoplifting. It was an especially poor choice for shoplifting a giant bag of marshmallows.

I'd already grown cocky when it came to shoplifting. My parents had moved us to Roseville from Corona, California a couple of years prior, and if Roseville, a suburb of Sacramento, wasn't dreadfully boring enough as it was (I called it Mayberry upon arriving, but soon found out it lacked even Mayberry's charm, neither city nor country, just a storage space for people and the fast-food restaurants that fed them), the move also split our family in half. My three older brothers stayed behind. There were other weirdos at Roseville high, but not the right flavor of weirdo and I found it very difficult to make friends. So, with only one brother left, who was five years younger than me, and a few friends, I desperately clung to an abusive friendship with a bully named Jim. Jim was a giant of a kid who had also just moved to Roseville, from San Antonio, Texas.

He and I fancied ourselves sophisticated bad boys amongst the rubes, and one of our favorite bad boy activities was shoplifting. I did most of the actual theft, with Jim there to cheer me on. Mail fraud was more his speed or so he said. He may have just been a spoiled rich kid whose parents were early adopters of shopping by mail.

I was sure I could shoplift anything from anywhere while wearing anything. I was somewhat justified in this arrogance; I made weekly trips to lift donuts from this very Bel Air, and I must say, it was a pretty masterful heist each time. I would saunter up to the bakery counter, and a clerk in a brown plastic apron would help me out, putting the donuts I pointed to into a pink box.

Friendly and smiling, I'd engage in small talk as I selected twelve donuts, "Just having a lazy Sunday with the family. Might go see the Robocop at the $2 movies later."

The clerk would invite me to choose one more donut. This is what's known as a baker's dozen; it turns out that when you steal twelve donuts, they give you an extra one for free.

He'd offer to ring me up and I'd say, "No, thank you. I have to grab a few other items. My mom hears I'm heading to Bel Air and out comes the list. You know how it is."

I'd take my pink box of sweet fried dough and walk past the cashiers and through the automatic opening doors. And the bakery clerk would have assumed I'd be paying the cashiers, because, really, who would have the audacity to have someone box up items they were stealing from them? And Jim and I would have delicious fresh donuts. We'd even share the booty with Jim's parents, such sweet boys we were to bring them donuts on a weekend morning.

Regular shoplifting benefited from the same kind of nerve. Just do it quickly and go, no pacing about nervously, that's how you get caught. It was all about momentum and confidence.

With this strategy in mind, and Jim waiting outside, I walked up, grabbed the big pillow-like package of marshmallows, put the half of it that fit under my jacket, and headed to the door. All with no hesitation, no stopping to look at the greeting cards, and no going into the bathroom to try to situate the contraband better under my jacket. One of the under-cover security guys stood at the door waiting for me.

The undercovers at a supermarket can't nab you until you walk through the door. You haven't actually stolen anything until you exit the building without paying for it. This can be a source of great fun. The next time you're doing your shopping, wear clothes with a lot of pockets and stuff them with everything you need, just load them pockets on up. By the time you're done, you'll have every under-cover in the place following you. Go get in line at the check-stand, unload your pockets onto the belt, and pay with a smile. You can delight in the disappointed looks on their faces, and feel good that you kept them distracted thus assisting any actual shoplifters now able to ply their trade unhindered.

Normally the undercovers stand near the doors inconspicuously as they wait for their prey to attempt an exit, casually reading a magazine, or looking at the latest artistic masterpiece sculpted from cases of soda to match whatever season we're in, be it the jack-o-lantern made from cases of Orange Crush for Halloween, or the rare unity of Coke and Pepsi working together to form a patriotic display for the Fourth of July. Normally the undercovers try to remain, well, undercover. Normally, but on this occasion, as I made my way to the door with a marshmallow-stuffed plastic pillow sticking out of my tiny proto-hipster leather jacket, the security guard stood in plain sight. Heading into middle age with feathered, peroxide-enhanced blonde hair and that carefully maintained unshaven look that Don Johnson on Miami Vice had made popular a few years earlier, he stood blocking the door and shaking his head as if to say, "C'mon kid, don't do this." Because honestly, who wants to be the dude busting the special little guy trying to hide a giant sack of marshmallows under his tiny leather coat?

But, momentum is a powerful thing, and though I saw him, and made eye contact with him even, I quickly turned to my left and walked through the next set of doors over.

With an exasperated sigh, he stepped through the door and put a hand on my shoulder, "All right, kid. Let's go."

I considered running. I thought Jim, who I could see staring at me open-mouthed, might have run interference, pretending to trip, and blocking my pursuer. If it had been one of the older undercovers I might have chanced it, but Don Johnson here looked like he might be up to the chase, like it'd give him something to talk about at the singles bar later. And I wasn't sure I could count on Jim to do anything, after all, why was he waiting outside yet again while I took all the risks? My heart was pounding just standing still, which also made running seem like a poor prospect. Fight or flight both gave way to freeze and hope for the best.

I was taken to the back warehouse part of the store, past the bathrooms and employee lockers to a windowless office.

While I waited for the store manager, various clerks peeked in at me, and they laughed as they filled each other in. "Marshmallows? Really? Marshmallows. Wow. He looks so sweet."

And I did look so sweet. I heard it all the time. I heard it from the principal's secretary in elementary school after seeing me in the office for the fourth time that week. I heard it from my friends' parents as they decided whether or not to let their kids continue hanging out with me. I heard it from my aunt as she consoled my poor suffering mother after various detentions, suspensions, and other heart-breaks. No matter how I tried to cultivate a *Rebel Without a Cause* look, a brooding, dangerous image, I always came across as *so sweet*. Of course, I was more than happy to use this when it would serve me.

Sitting in the grocery store manager's drab, claustrophobic office I practiced looking sweet, and scared, and sad, and like I definitely had learned my lesson. Eventually, a heavy-set man with thinning hair, a wide tie, and a short-sleeved shirt came in and took a seat facing me.

"Kid, we're going to do you a favor. We're going to call your mom instead of the police."

This was no favor, and definitely not the sympathetic response I'd hoped for. I'd sooner face life behind bars than see the disappointment and concern on my mother's face. My mom grew up working-class poor living in various apartments in Brooklyn, rough and tough 1950s Brooklyn, not the gentrified burrow it is today, and yet somehow mom remained an angel, a rough and tough angel. As a child, my mom dreamed of being a nun. She even went to nun camp. Who knew nun camp was a thing? It's a thing, or at least it was back when my mom was a kid. She has a framed photograph on her nightstand of her and her sister dressed in nun's habits posing with adult nuns as if they were little league baseball players posing with their big league heroes.

At some point, my mom, a stunningly pretty young woman with blonde hair and a sharp sense of style, gave up her nun aspirations and set her sights on having a bunch of kids so that she could give them a better childhood than she had. A life with a stable, supportive home life, in a house with a yard. This was her greatest desire, and on paper she achieved it, but the universe with its vicious sense of humor saw fit to give my mom five loud, hyperactive, constantly fighting, delinquents for sons.

Every time I or my brothers committed any sort of minor childhood hijinks, skipping school, sampling candy from the bulk bins at the grocery store, forging our parent's signatures on notes from our teachers, she was sure that it was the beginning of a life of crime destined to end in the electric chair.

One of the many psychiatrists I shared time with as a kid commented to my mom that "Kids like Keith..." (and I always loved this phrase, as it implied there were more out there like me. I dream of finding this lost tribe of Kids like Keith but they remain elusive.) "Kids like Keith—" he warned. "—tend to hit one extreme or another, either achieving great success or ending up in serious trouble with the law."

He did me no favors putting this idea in mom's head, reinforcing her fear that I was bound for a life of crime. And now, here I was, an actual criminal, caught red-handed stealing marshmallows.

Mom's minivan pulled up in front of the store, and the manager, embarrassed for both of us, walked me out. Nobody called out "Dead Man Walking" but that was the feeling that hung in the air. We're Catholic. I hear Catholic moms have a special talent for guilt, but I hear Jewish mothers excel at this as well, same with Italian mothers, Irish mothers, and Mexican mothers. I'm pretty convinced the power to evoke overpowering feelings of guilt is a universal maternal trait. We drove home in silence. Mom got out of the van without saying a word. I went straight up to my room to wait for my father to get home.

Dad also grew up in Brooklyn. Unlike my mom, my father was no angel. He hustled. The nuns my mom so adored rapped dad's knuckles with rulers. He wore black-framed glasses, had thick dark brown, almost black, hair, and he's worn the same bright, mischievous smile since he was a baby. He started smoking when still in his single digits, and made his own money shining shoes, peddling ice cream on the beach, and selling newspapers to drunks in bars, making himself a little tip with each transaction by claiming he was unable to make change. My dad was the kind of kid who'd grow up to knock up the girl who once wanted to become a nun. That isn't quite an accurate description of what happened, just a technically correct one and a pretty fair description of my father.

I was worried. I was scared. Dad was going to be mad.

Dad's unfortunate messaging, (perhaps unintentionally

though maybe not), was that he was mostly pissed at us for getting caught.

Our talks were less about right and wrong and more along the lines of, "You got caught so take your damn punishment. Don't like it? Don't get caught."

There were times when he tempered my mom's border-line hysterical response to our delinquency. On one occasion he came home from work, ready to slip his shoes off and get lost in a Stephen King novel in the "nice living room," the one spot in our home where rough housing and rowdiness were strictly off-limits, only to be told that he had to first administer a spanking to me for one sin or another.

He walked me into the master bedroom, shut the door and took off his belt. I waited with dread for him to sit so I could assume the proper spanking receiving position, bent over his lap.

Instead, he said to me gruffly, "Make it sound real or it will be," and he gave his dresser three sharp slaps with the belt. I howled in agony, really doing it up, going for the Oscar.

He shot me a "Don't overdo it" look and he went to the nice living room to finish the last few chapters of *Pet Sematary*.

This was not likely to be an occasion for my dad to see it my way. Not stealing, and certainly not getting caught steal-ing, were pretty high on dad's list of personal command-ments. After what felt like forever I heard his car pull into the driveway. There was a pause as Mom filled him in on the day's catastrophes, and then the sound of his heavy foot-steps coming up the stairs.

Thump, thump, thump, thump, then down the hall, *THUMP, THUMP, THUMP THUMP*. My doom getting closer and closer, my heart beating louder and louder in my chest as his foot-steps came closer.

My door opened, and he said two words, two words that summed up everything that needed to be said. "Fucking marshmallows?"

And I laughed. This was a frequent problem. When I was in trouble, I laughed. This sometimes got me out of fights. It sometimes got me into fights. It usually got me in more trouble than I was already in, but with my dad, thankfully, there was understanding.

He'd respond, "I know you laugh when you're scared, and you should be scared because you're in deep shit."

And he'd go on yelling, not flummoxed by my giggles.

"Marshmallows, Keith? Really? Big, puffy, bright white, awkward, no resale value, marshmallows? I'd understand jewelry or cash, but fucking marshmallows?"

"I'll try to do better next time," I mumbled.

"THAT'S NOT WHAT I'M SAYING AND YOU GODDAMN KNOW IT!" he bellowed.

I told him I wouldn't do it again, that it was my first time.

"Your first time? Really? Bullshit! Isn't it funny how people always get caught on their first time?" he sneered.

"Well, it makes sense actually. You're nervous and inexperienced, and…"

"YOU WANNA KEEP SMART-ASSING ME!?"

I didn't. I mean, I kind of wanted to compliment him on the verb form of "smart-ass," knowing that if I managed to make him laugh it could sometimes lessen the punishment, but I decided it was better not to risk it.

Dad struggled to wrap his head around why his supposedly gifted son continued to be such an idiot time and time again, and I needed to give him a reasonable explanation for why I had tried to smuggle a trash bag sized bag of fluffed-up bright white sugar cushions out of a grocery store in broad daylight. A lightbulb went off in my brain and I saw a way forward. I'd live to be an idiot again.

"It was a dare, dad." He froze.

He could tip either way. More was needed.

"I know it was stupid, but that was kind of the point. Jim dared me to do it and I went for it."

I didn't mind throwing Jim under the bus. He'd done

nothing when the security guard grabbed me. Jim was huge for his age, and often posed as my adult big brother to get us into R-rated movies. He could have at least tried talking to the security guard, or to the store manager. He just split for home the minute he saw the guy escorting me by the shoulder back into the store. And besides, my dad already hated Jim.

Dad's angry face softened slightly.

"You're right. That is stupid," he responded, and he left, satisfied with my explanation.

And it was twenty years before I admitted to him, from onstage at a comedy show, that there had been no dare, just two teenagers with a bad case of the munchies who decided they needed some Rice Krispy treats but only had the Rice Krispies.

CHRISTIAN

On my 18th birthday, I signed a rental agreement on an apartment in Midtown Sacramento, California, moving out of my parents' home for the second time. On both occasions, my roommate was Christian Gibson, a hard-drinking artist I'd first become friends with at Success High, a continuation school that is the modern equivalent of a reform school.

Christian was a handsome Native American, with dark features and thick black hair which he kept shorn on the sides, and spikey on top, a hairdo he jokingly called "The Love Rhino." He fit in with the long-haired, heavy metal loving kids at Success High even less than I did. When he walked away from the benches where most of us had our lunch and instead sat by himself in the middle of the basketball court in the sun, unselfconsciously spreading out a cloth napkin for his lunch of French bread, brie cheese, and sparkling water, I knew we'd be friends. We bonded over art, poetry, and music, and we discovered together the wonders of alcohol.

By the time we moved into one of the ground-level flats of a fourplex in Midtown Sacramento, our hobby of drinking had become an all-consuming passion. I spent the first two months of my legal adulthood getting drunk everyday with

Christian, working various jobs while hungover and collecting recyclables from trash cans when the alcohol funds ran low.

Worried that I was becoming an alcoholic, I quit drinking abruptly, which Christian took as a personal insult. He became increasingly surly toward me. I gave notice on the one-bedroom apartment we shared with one other room-mate and started the countdown to when we'd all move out. I'd be taking up residence on a friend's couch a few blocks over and restarting my adulthood. In the final week, things grew especially tense between us roommates, and I slowly checked off the days.

I was on the couch watching the giant wooden cabinet TV set we'd dragged in after it had been abandoned in some alley when suddenly the front door crashed open. Christian barged in, wasted and spoiling for a fight. He was a talented skateboarder and despite the heavy drinking one of the more athletic people I knew. I was taller than him by almost half a foot, but he had muscles and broad shoulders while I was lean and lanky. We'd speculated about which of us would win in a fight, the way boys do, and he chose this night to find out. I was pretty sure on most days the answer would be him, but on this night he was drunk, sloppy drunk, past the liquid courage, anesthetizing stage where it can be an advantage, and I was sober.

"Come here. I wanna fight you," he stated, matter of factly as he made his way toward me.

I jumped behind the couch. He made his way around it and I ran in the other direction to the front door. He had shut and locked the door behind him. I got the lock undone just as he lunged at me, and back around the couch we went. Passing the door for the second time, I managed to open it before starting our orbit around the couch yet again. I was on my way to the entryway of the fourplex we lived in, with one more set of doors to get through before I'd be outside. I was hoping the doors were open lest I be caught in a small space with a drunk maniac. I was in luck, Christian had left these doors wide open. But before I could make it through them, Christian managed to get a hold of me. I used our momentum to swing him around in front of me, spin him, and put him in a chokehold.

I didn't want to kill him, I just wanted to not be killed by him, and he scared the hell out of me, so I kept on him like a bull rider at a rodeo, until the lack of oxygen slowed him down. As soon as he stopped trying to buck me off of him I let go and headed for that open door. To my amazement, he was up and at me again by the time I hit the sidewalk running.

I found a couch to crash on for the night and headed home in the morning. Christian was waiting, standing in the middle of the living room in dark sunglasses.

I said, "Good morning" as I entered the apartment, and he slowly slid his shades down revealing that the whites of both of his eyes were almost completely red.

"You did this to me," he said as if he expected me to feel bad.

"Yeah, I did that to you in self-defense," I replied, and I started laughing, my usual nervous laughing, and having to excuse this laughter somehow, I quickly summoned up a joke.

"And also, it looks cool as hell. And you know it looks cool. You went and found dark sunglasses and practiced sliding 'em down your face like that because you know just how cool it looks."

He didn't see the humor.

"My mom is coming to take me to see a doctor," he informed me, trying again to make me feel guilty.

I'd felt just how strong he was and I stood there sure that sober, he'd mop the floor with me easily, but psychology is a big part of fighting. Though he didn't remember the night before very well, he knew that he'd come out of it looking worse than I did. We stared at each other. It remained a standstill.

His mom honked her horn, and he headed out.

"Tell Sheila I say hello," I shouted after him.

As I started to clean up the trashed living room the phone rang.

"Hello," I answered.

"Hello, this is the Sacramento Police Department, is Christian Gibson there?"

That rat had called the police on me? "No, he's not here right now. Can I help you?"

"He called to report an assault," she said, sounding bored.

"Oh, yeah that. He had a fight with our roommate. They're all better now. In fact they just went out to lunch together with Christian's mom," I lied.

"That would be Keith Jensen?"

"Yep, that's the guy. They're probably at Taco Bell right now. Should I have Christian call you when he gets back?"

She was sounding increasingly annoyed at having to talk to me. "Do you know if he still wants to press charges? Do we need to send an officer out?"

I considered telling her what my favorite order at Taco Bell was (a seven layer burrito, no sour cream, no cheese).

"Oh, no, no. He and Keith are all made up. No, need," I assured her.

"Okay then, tell him to call us if he changes his mind."

"Yes. I will tell him. I will be sure to give him that message," I lied again.

And that is how one drops the charges on one's self.

I WANT TO RIDE MY BICYCLE

It was a gorgeous Sacramento evening, the delta breeze was blowing in the lovely way it does, making it almost worth the horrible heat one must suffer through before they can properly appreciate it. I left the Crest Theater where my sketch comedy troupe, "I Can't Believe It's Not Comedy" had just finished rehearsing in the basement. Rehearsal had gone very well, and combined with the perfect weather, I was feeling great as I pedaled my way toward a local bar where I'd be performing a stand-up comedy set. In fact, I was in such a good mood I was steering back and forth carving left to right and left again across my lane.

"Pull over!" a loud voice demanded.

I looked over my shoulder and saw that the cop yelling at me to pull over was also on a bicycle, a stern look on his mustachioed face.

"Pull over!" he barked again, and I started to laugh.

Thinking back, I'm unsure if this was my usual nervous laughing, or genuine laughter, because being pulled over on your bike, by a cop on their bike, is funny; even the phrase "Pull over" strikes me as funny when applied to a bicycle.

I'm a comedian. I like to have fun.

So I considered yelling back at him that I knew the rules and wouldn't pull over unless he made the siren noises,

"Wooooooh, wooooooh!" but then I remembered that cops tend not to have a sense of humor so I just pulled over instead.

The cop did exactly as he would have if we had both been in motor vehicles, which is to say he parked behind me, his headlight shining on the back of my head, and made me wait what seemed like a really long time. I had a comedy gig to get to! I couldn't imagine what I was waiting for. I knew he wasn't running my plates through his dashboard computer since I didn't have plates, and he didn't have a dashboard.

Eventually, his backup buddy came flying around the corner. This second cop was thin, so thin I was immediately reminded of the scene in The Muppet Movie where Kermit the Frog rides a bike, and it just doesn't look right, seeming to break a law or two of physics. On his face was a pair of big, stereotypical motorcycle cop glasses. He parked next to the first cop, and they swung their legs over their back tires together in a perfectly synchronized motion that might have looked kind of badass, had they been on motorcycles and wearing long pants.

They walked toward me, Sunglasses stopped a few feet away and fixed a stare on me in a way that said we might have a failure to communicate. The original cop, we'll call him Mustache, stepped up to me on my bike.

"You know why I pulled you over?" he asked, and again I laughed. "Is something funny?"

Having nervous laughter all my life, I'd learned that rather than explaining this affliction to teachers, employers, and cops, it was better just to come up with something funny to excuse the laughter. "Well, I've just never been 'pulled over' on my bike before. It strikes me as funny that we're both on bicycles like we're kids playing *traffic stop*."

"I assure you, this isn't a game. Do you know why I pulled you over?" he asked again, confirming my early thought about cops and their lack of a sense of humor.

Another giggle slipped out before I replied, "Because I

was riding on K street? To be fair, I was really just crossing K street diagonally. You see, I was just at The Crest and..."

"YOU WERE RIDING ON K STREET!" he barked much with rage and spittle.

"Okay, fine. You can give me a ticket then. Just calm down!"

I told a cop to calm down. If I have any wisdom to impart from my experiences in this life, any contribution to the sum of human knowledge it is this; never tell a cop to calm down. Telling a cop to calm down has the opposite of its intended effect.

"I'M PERFECTLY CALM!" he yelled with much rage and irony, and still more spittle. "You were riding on K Street."

K Street in downtown Sacramento is a weird street. In the time I've lived here it's been a pedestrian-only mall, an actual shopping mall, then open to bikes, and finally half of it was swallowed by an arena and the rest was opened to cars in a limited capacity. Light rail tracks ran down the middle of the street, and there were planters with bricks affixed diagonally on them creating spikes so that you couldn't sit on them, as the city was keen to make sure they didn't accidentally give any homeless people rest or comfort. I happened to be riding my bike during the time when K Street was reserved for pedestrians and light rail trains only.

I was done being yelled at over something so trivial. "Look, you think I was, I don't agree. Write me a ticket, and I'll sign it. I'll probably even pay it. We don't have to agree and we don't have to like each other. It's really not a big deal, hardly the crime of the century, right?"

"Do you have a driver's license?" he asked, still sounding like he suspected me of something awful like puppy murder or toddler taunting.

"I don't need a driver's license. I'm riding a bike," I answered with a smirk.

"Do you have *any* identification!" he said through gritted teeth.

"Yeah," I answered, handing him my driver's license.
"Have you ever been arrested, Mr. Jensen?"

"Ah, come on. Do I have to answer that? Over a traffic
stop, a *bicycle* traffic stop?" I remembered that I hadn't both-
ered to have the charges of assaulting a peace officer and
resisting arrest expunged from my record and started to
regret this decision.

"Yes. You have to answer my questions."

"Yeah, I've been arrested a few times."

"Surprise, surprise. What for?"

"...assaulting a police officer," I mumbled.

"What was that?!"

"I was arrested for assaulting a peace officer."

"Why am I not surprised?"

"I don't know, man. You should be. I'm a solid citizen
who is just trying to enjoy a bike ride."

"Right."

Mustache went back to his bike to radio in my license
and to make sure I didn't have any outstanding warrants, or
any fantastic or totally rad warrants either. His buddy
Sunglasses stayed with the suspect, arms folded across his
chest, lifeless mirrored sunglasses stare fixed on me. It was
at this time that it occurred to me that this was going to
make a great story. I started to compose the Facebook post
in my head. I decided what I needed to really put it over the
top were some pictures. I reached into my pocket and slid
out my old clamshell cell phone. I snapped a picture of each
of the two cops.

"What are you doing?" Sunglasses asked.

"I was just getting a couple of pictures, to remember our
time together," I answered.

"You can't take our picture."

"Like fuck I can't."

"Give me the phone," he demanded.

"Go fuck yourself," I answered, incensed at his unreason-
able demand and feeling it enough to have overpowered all
instincts for self-preservation.

Sunglasses grabbed me by the wrist, and I snapped my hand away from him.

"Get your goddamn hands off of me!" I yelled.

And that was it. He put both his hands on me, used his foot to sweep my legs out from under me, and bounced me off of the ground, knocking the wind out of me. His buddy came running.

"Oh yeah, here we go!" he yelled, like an excited spectator at a sporting event.

I tasted blood in my mouth. This area of downtown was where the nicer hotels were, and at just that moment a wedding photographer rounded the corner with his camera already out and ready.

Spotting the two cops and me, thinking, "Oh shit, a Pulitzer!" he jumped into action, getting right in close.

Funny thing; the cops didn't mind *him* taking their pictures. They were posing like a couple of hunters with a fresh kill. With my arms wrenched behind me and a cop's knee in my back, blood on my teeth and lips, I looked up at him as his camera clicked away.

"Hi. My name is Keith Lowell Jensen. I would love to have copies of these photographs," I managed to say, not because I was thinking about the value the pictures might have in court later but rather because I'm a comedian and good headshots are expensive.

The cops got me to my feet. Sunglasses still had on his sunglasses, they weren't even askew. For such a skinny guy he was remarkably strong, and at the moment quite proud of himself, trying to restrain a shit-eating grin that threatened to overtake his cool cop mystique.

Mustache meanwhile had gone full Barney Fife, bouncing around like a madman. "You're under arrest. You sure are stupid. I'd decided I was gonna let you go with a warning, but now you're going to jail. How do you like that? You excited about spending the night in jail? You excited about being under arrest and going to jail? Is that funny to you?"

I took a few deep breaths. Not covering my disdain for him.

I said, "Yeah, I get it. I'm going to jail. Cool. Can I ask one question?"

"What's that?"

"How?"

He returned my hateful glare. "I mean, I've been arrested before but never by a dude on a bicycle. Do I get on your handlebars? Are we gonna act out that scene from ET? Or do I have to run behind?"

"We'll call a car to come get you," he answered through gritted teeth, his earlier enthusiasm dampening.

"Oh, you have to call car cops," I replied. "That must be so humiliating for you."

We stared at each other for a long thirty seconds. He gave up on a comeback and pulled out his radio to call a car. I would not be making it to my gig.

The cop car showed up pretty quick, driving right down the middle of the K Street pedestrian mall, and parking right there, on the light rail tracks. Two car cops got out and talked to the two bike cops.

The car cops came to fetch me and I said, "Hey, what happens to my bike?"

"We'll put it in the trunk," one of them answered, sounding bored.

"I think you'd better look at my bike." It was a ridiculous stretched-out Dyno-cruiser with springer forks and extra-wide handlebars.

"Yeah. That isn't gonna fit in our trunk," the car cop observed.

So, the car cops, who'd been called by the bike cops, called some truck cops to come get my bike, and the truck cops drove their cop truck right down the middle of the K Street pedestrian mall, and parked behind the car cops' cop car, smack bang on the light rail tracks all in the name of protecting the mall from me and my bicycle.

My bike was loaded up and carted off to bike jail. I was

loaded up into the cop car, and the two bike cops ran to their bikes and got into position like they were getting ready for the Tour De France to kick off.

The car cops slid into their vehicle and the one behind the wheel looked at me in the rearview mirror and by way of greeting asked, "Hey man, don't ya just hate bike cops?"

"I DO!" I laughed. "I really do. I mean, to be fair, I normally don't like you guys either, but hey, the enemy of my enemy is my friend so I'm cool with you guys tonight."

"Look at 'em," he said, motioning at the two officers in shorts. "They're gonna try to race us to the jail now. It's their big thrill. You doing anything tonight?"

"Me? Nah, man, not anymore. Just going to jail."

"You wanna drive around a while?"

"Yeah, that sounds awesome." I laughed, and we took a lovely trip around the State Capital Building.

We cruised by the California Museum where there was a reception for the Charles Shultz exhibit.

"Dude, check it out, it's Arnold!" The cop in the passenger seat pointed out the former Mr. Universe, current actor, and future Governator.

He talked more smack on bike cops. "Did you know those guys volunteer for that? When I joined up I was worried I'd get stuck on a bike, but no, those dudes are just clamoring to look like that, and to go around harassing skateboarders."

I laughed hard at this, having often been chased out of a favorite skate spot by cops on bikes.

I chanced a joke. "Hey, you guys think the cops in the truck are joking around with my bike right now about how much they hate car cops?"

I got a laugh and so I took a chance. "Hey, I'm actually supposed to be performing stand-up comedy right now, just a few blocks from here. You know what would be really funny? If you guys took me to my gig. You can even leave the handcuffs on."

This got another laugh. And then they took me to jail, after a quick stop for frozen yogurt.

Despite missing my gig I was having about as much fun as one can have in the back of a cop car in a set of painfully tight handcuffs.

When we did finally get to the jail the bicyclists were there waiting, leaning against a wall, trying to look casual. I giggled at the thought of them trying to hold that position while we drove all over town.

Before letting me out, the cop behind the steering wheel turned to me again. "Can I give you some advice?"

"Yeah, sure."

"I know you're mad, but you need to calm down and not let these guys get to you. They hold all the power right now. You play it cool, you spend one night in jail and you maybe get a small fine. You keep fighting with these dudes, this could be a pain in your ass for a long time to come."

"You're right. Thanks."

They let me out, and I immediately apologized to the bike buddies. "Hey guys, I lost my temper back there. I'm sorry. I've had a chance to calm down now and I'm going to cooperate from here on out."

"All right. That's good to hear. Thank you," Mustache replied, and then he walked me into the jail.

He was still arresting me as if we hadn't just become buds.

I was fingerprinted and tested for tuberculosis. The TB test is a nice freebie you get when you go to jail.

In a last ditch, Hail Mary attempt to not spend the night in jail and maybe still make my gig, I told them I needed to take medication every night for my Ulcerative Colitis. Which is true.

"What happens if you don't take it?" they asked.

I answered, "Shit and blood everywhere." Which is not true.

All this got me was an orange plastic ID bracelet instead of the usual white.

Mustache handed me over to the biggest man I'd ever seen in my life up to that point. This huge giant of a dude stood in his tight-fitting police uniform waiting to receive me and he looked... hungry.

"What's this one in for?" he asked the bicyclist.

"We picked him up on a 148," Mustache answered.

"A 1 4 8, huh?" Gigantor repeated, savoring each syllable.

"Yeah, a 148, but with remorse."

"With remorse?" the giant repeated, sounding disappointed. "Okay."

I don't speak cop but I'm pretty sure this odd exchange was the bike cop telling the giant jail cop that I was being cool now so he shouldn't be too rough with me, and the giant was sad about it.

Gigantor took me through to where the cells were. He put me face-first against a wall and instructed me to keep my nose on the wall while taking off my socks.

I could not do this, and several times he yelled, "KEEP YOUR NOSE ON THE WALL!"

Then I finally yelled back, "I CAN'T KEEP MY NOSE ON THE WALL AND TAKE MY SOCKS OFF! IT'S ONE OR THE OTHER."

He laughed at me and told me to hurry up and get my socks off, turn 'em inside out and shake them and put them back on. I did so, and he walked me down a hallway. I knew the drunk tank, having walked past it on previous occasions. I was surprised when we stopped there, and the door opened.

"I'm sorry, there seems to be some confusion. This is the drunk tank. I'm not drunk. I don't even drink. I was riding my bike in the mall," I said.

"You got that," he replied, pointing at my snazzy new medical alert bracelet.

"Because I have a medical condition I have to go to the drunk tank?"

"It's the closest cell to us, in case we need to respond because you start dying."

And he put his hand on my arm and moved me into the cell. "Sit. You sit down in this cell."

The drunk tank had no furniture, no metal benches, just a low sidewalk around the perimeter of the cell with a gently sloping curbside. I looked around and most of my new temporary roommates were sitting on the sidewalk, a few were lying on the floor, or sitting cross-legged. There was a metal toilet in the room with no seat and no privacy. I knew that I would piss myself before using that toilet.

I looked around. There was an interesting-looking guy in the corner and I decided to sit by him and strike up a conversation. I figured if I had to spend the night in the drunk tank I might at least try to get a good story out of it, and then this would be a work trip.

As soon as I sat down he asked me, "What time is it?" with some urgency.

"It's probably around 9:30 or 10," I answered.

"Shit. I gotta get out of here by midnight or that bitch is gonna sell my rims."

I tried my best to relate, "What is it with bitches always trying to sell a dude's rims?"

He gave me a look that said he thought I was making fun of him and I started to feel guilty because I was kind of making fun of him. "Sorry, man. You got some nice rims, eh?"

"Yeah. They're $2,000 rims."

"Oh shit. What kind of car you got?"

"What? I ain't got no car. I just got rims."

"Dude! You could score a running Toyota Corolla for $2,000."

"What? I don't want a fuckin' Corolla."

"Yeah, okay. Sorry." I didn't tell him that I was quite happy with my Toyota Corolla. "You seem pretty sober. I bet they'll get you out of here before midnight."

"God's gonna take care of me. I know that much."

Now, I'm not the kind of atheist who needs to push it on people, despite what you may have heard. I'm outspoken about it, but I'm not knocking on anyone's door. Generally, if you want to hear my religious beliefs you've got to come to me, and probably pay a cover, and there's a two-drink minimum too.

But I was here hoping for a story, and bored, and so I said, "Well, what makes you so sure. I mean, God doesn't seem to be taking such good care of us right now. What makes you so sure he's got our backs, if he even exists?"

Rims looked at me with a look I will never forget. I suddenly became very aware of being the only white guy in the cell, wearing a collared shirt and a wool trench coat. I have never felt more like Satan himself. Rims moved away from me without a word.

The door opened and Gigantor was back but he was no longer the biggest man I'd ever seen. I was amazed to see this mountain of a cop pushing an even larger man into the cell.

He took the cuffs off, and said his line, "Sit down! You sit in this cell."

The new inmate, a black man with a bodybuilder physique, on display as he wasn't wearing a shirt, looked back at Officer Gigantor and said, firmly, "I can't sit down. I'm drunk."

"You'll sit down. You sit in this cell."

"I TOLD YOU I CAN'T SIT DOWN OR I'LL FUCKING PUKE!"

"YOU SIT IN THIS CELL," the cop ordered, placing his hand on his nightstick.

The Bodybuilder balled up his fists. The rest of us moved to the far corners of the room because if these two fought, it was hard to imagine we'd come out unscathed, or even alive. If these two men fought, I was sure the building would be coming down around us.

I thought about trying to intervene and advising Gigantor that it might be best to listen to The Bodybuilder when he says he's drunk. I mean we didn't know where he was in his spin cycle and if he started puking I'm guessing he wouldn't be cleaning up after himself. I stayed quiet.

The Bodybuilder stared at the cop, flexing his chest muscles intimidatingly.

The cop stared at the bodybuilder... and then he did something he'd probably not done many times in his life. He backed down.

He took his hands off his nightstick, and he said, "Fine. The rest of you sit in this cell."

Then he walked back through the door which clanged shut behind him.

The Bodybuilder was already an intimidating man, but seeing the Paul Bunyon cop back down to him, well he was like a god now as he paced in the middle of the cell, a domain that was now his.

Rims was the first to speak to him, "Hey man, you know what time it is?"

He focused on Rims and said, loud and matter-of-factly "It's 3 o'clock in the goddamn morning!"

And with this, my buddy Rims started crying, sobbing in fact.

"Oh shit, shit, that bitch has sold my rims for sure. Shit."

I tried to comfort him. "Hey, dude, it's cool. There's no way, it's 3 in the morning man. I left rehearsal around 5 and it took 'em a while to decide to arrest me, they had to get a car, and a truck, and then we drove around a little, there's a Charles Schultz exhibit at the California Museum, Arnold Schwarzenegger was there, and then I was put in here with you because I told 'em I might shit myself, and so it's not past midnight. There's no way."

I was trying to speak softly, but apparently The Bodybuilder had muscular eardrums too.

"The fuck did you just say?" he barked at me.

"What? Oh, um, yeah, my friend here, see he's worried about his rims which he'll lose at midnight, sort of a

Cinderella kind of deal I guess, haha, and well, I know what time I was arrested and like I was telling him, we drove around a bit, and did you know there's a Charles Schultz exhibit at the California Museum? You like Snoopy?"

"You telling me what time it is?!" Rage showed on his face as his fist once again balled up.

I started to think there might be blood and shit to clean up for real. I started laughing, not just nervous giggling, but full-on panic laughing.

"Something funny, bitch?"

I pondered explaining that I laughed when scared, but instead I said, "Well, yeah."

"Why don't you tell me what's so goddamn funny?"

And continuing to laugh I managed to get out, "Well, you're asking me if I'm telling you what time it is, which is an expression, but you mean it literally and I am in fact, literally telling you what time it is, and this strikes me as very funny."

"Oh, so you're a comedian?" and with this I started to howl. "And now what's so funny?"

"I AM! HA HA HA! I am a comedian! That's literally what I do for a living, I'm a comedian, and right now I'm a comedian telling you what time it is, and this is how I'm gonna die, and this is such an appropriate, even poetic, death for a comedian. I've made my peace with it."

And with this, The Bodybuilder sat down between me and Rims, and he put his arm around me, and he announced to the whole cell, "Hey everybody, we got us a goddamn comedian. Tell us some jokes, funny man."

All the men in the cell gathered around and I spent the next hour telling jokes to drunk people, which is perfect because that's all I'd been trying to do with my night to begin with.

PUBLIC DEFENDING 101

It's always fun walking into work late with the excuse that you just got out of jail. I've had a lot of jobs, which isn't uncommon for anyone working in the arts but when I took a job in the office of a roofing company I got stuck. I couldn't seem to get fired and it was just too convenient and flexible for me to justify quitting.

My boss Dave, hearing me say, "Sorry I'm late. I just got out of jail," immediately called Rick, Kevin, and Bob into the room. Any time he sensed a good story was coming, he'd call a meeting like this. I told them the whole sordid tale about Mustache and Sunglasses, the bike cops, and drunk tank and of course The Bodybuilder. Then the rest of the guys took turns telling their jail stories. Exchanging jail stories is right up there with fight stories, or showing off scars for some solid, masculine bonding.

Dave was walking his dog in the park by his house, he told us, when he heard a police helicopter overhead. They were looking for someone, and shining their searchlight down at the park, eventually landing on Dave. He had a flashlight in his hand for finding the dog shit and bagging it up in a little blue plastic bag, like a good citizen. He shined his light back up at the helicopter. The next thing he knew there were more flashlights in the park, shining in his face.

He had enough beers in him to think he could joke with the cops, after all he hadn't done anything wrong. "They told me my flashlight could have brought down their helicopter, so I said, 'If a flashlight could bring it down, maybe don't fly it over my fucking house anymore.' That's a fair point, isn't it?" We all had a good laugh, and agreed it was. This may be the real reason I stayed with this job. A boss who knows how to tell a goddamn story is a wonderful thing.

A few weeks later I met with the public defender because that's who I could afford to be defended by. It's been my experience that Public Defenders tend to be wonderful people. Reading the arresting officer's report she kept laughing and muttering, "Chicken shit. Such chicken shit." She was a delight, I liked her right away. "Ha, listen to this chicken shit. The officer says he took your phone because the police have been briefed on cell phones that can fire bullets!"

I laughed with her. "Oh wow, I don't have that app. I mean, to be fair if I never saw it in the app store I would definitely download it."

She continued to go over the report. I told her that the cops had gone into my phone and deleted the photos. "Yeah. They're chicken shit," was her reply. I was guessing this fact wasn't going to help my case.

When she finished reading the report she said, "I think you'll get your charges dropped, Mr. Jensen. This report is chicken shit. You won't even have to go before the judge. I'll get this thrown out."

I was glad to hear this. "Can I ask one question first? What was I arrested for? What was my charge?"

"Resisting arrest," she answered.

"And what else?"

"Nothing, just resisting arrest."

"Right, but what was I being arrested for when I resisted?"

"Nothing. That's the whole charge, resisting arrest."

"So I was arrested for resisting being arrested for resisting being arrested for resisting being arrested?"

"Yes."

"What the fuck is that, the Moebius Strip of Arrests?"

She liked this. "Ha. The Moebius Strip of Arrests. That's funny. Want me to say that to the judge?"

"Um… I don't know. I mean, you're the one who passed the bar, but I'm not sure this is the best time for you to be practicing your tight five. I can take you to some open mic nights if you want to try comedy. Maybe you should just say lawyery things like precedence, and jurisprudence."

"No, this judge will love it. He's a pisser."

"Uh… okay, I guess?"

With my blessing she went in to talk to this pisser of a judge armed with my joke. A few minutes later was back with a smile on her face.

All charges were dropped.

FAMOUS

I was back at The Crest Theatre a week or two after having been arrested and leaving there on my bike. I was picking up my wife, who worked at The Crest as the box office manager. As I walked down K Street I saw the two bicyclists in cop shorts who'd arrested me. They were harassing homeless people for drinking in public, a ridiculous practice, as if the homeless wouldn't prefer to be drinking indoors somewhere, like maybe a bar, or better yet, a home; and fining people for being homeless is always a weird deal.

"So, you know how you have nothing, well we're gonna address that by making you have even less than nothing."

I met my wife in the lobby, and we went out the back door so I could warn the guys who usually drank in the alley that the bicyclists were shaking people down for open containers. There were four guys having beers, hurting no one. They thanked me for the heads up and put their bottles in their coats.

One of the guys, who was slightly less disheveled than the rest, turned to me and said, "Hey, I know you; you're a comedian."

It's always flattering to be recognized in public, especially in front of my wife.

"Yeah, I am," I responded. "Have you seen me at The Punch Line or maybe The Comedy Spot?"

"Dude, I was in jail with you. You're fucking hilarious."

My wife was very proud.

CHARLIE CHAPLIN

I love Charlie Chaplin. I've run into some younger folks who don't know who he is, and I can't be too mad about that, his best work was from almost a century ago. But even if they don't know who he is, they recognize pictures and clips, and so in service to one of my comedy heroes, and in service to any of you not yet familiar with his brilliant work, allow me to help you out.

You know those old films of Hitler dancing and singing? Well, that's actually Charlie Chaplin, a totally different guy who pissed off a lot of people by making a movie about how awful Hitler was way before knowing that Hitler was awful came into vogue. That confusion you felt at seeing history's most notorious warmonger and mass murderer seeming so jovial, and not a bad dancer either, well now you know, Charlie Chaplin. Same mustache, different guy. And for the record, Charlie had the mustache first. Hitler did a lot worse things of course, but among his crimes, he took from us the best comedy mustache of all time.

I recommend you watch some Chaplin. You can start with his early short films, but be sure you see The Kid, Modern Times, and The Great Dictator (the Hitler flick). And yeah, go ahead and watch the Robert Downey Jr. biopic if that'll help get you in the mood.

One more thing, get a kid to watch Chaplin with you. This isn't just because it's good for kids to be exposed to Chaplin, but also because kids will help you appreciate the depth and pathos Chaplin packed into his films. Kids ask questions.

I was watching Modern Times with my daughter when she was five and she asked, "Daddy, is Charlie a good guy or a bad guy?"

I answered, "I've always assumed he was a good guy. Why do you ask?"

"Charlie is always stealing food." She had a point.

Charlie's Little Tramp would sneak a sausage right out of a bun. The dude was a regular weenie wrangler. I wanted to give her a real answer, and not dumb it down.

I said, "Sweety, he's stealing food because he's hungry. That's not the same as stealing because you're greedy or lazy."

She looked thoughtful for a minute, before saying, "Okay, daddy," and we went back to watching the movie.

I was proud of her for getting it and proud of myself for not insulting her intelligence.

Then she asked, "Daddy, why are the cops so mean to Charlie?"

I wanted to give an equally honest answer, so I thought about it and I said, "Well, the thing is sweetheart, cops are dicks."

Please send my Father of the Year trophy to me via my publisher. It doesn't seem a good idea to give my address right about now.

In Modern Times, Charlie's Little Tramp character is arrested and my daughter was introduced to the concept of jail. It's a weird concept, jail. Like a human zoo with stripey pajamas.

"Where is he?" she asked.

"That's jail. He's in jail," I answered.

"What is jail?"

I realize here that we grew up with very different

cartoons. I don't remember learning what jail was. I watched Looney Tunes and saw the big bad wolf in jail, and Popeye also did a stretch in the big house. But my daughter was growing up watching Kipper the Dog and Thomas the Tank Engine, and neither of them ever spent time in the slammer. Dora the Explorer is pretty crafty but she never made a shiv that I know of.

So we're watching the Little Tramp scramble and hustle, trying to get a roof over his head, and something to eat through the whole movie, until finally he's arrested and put in jail where he's got a bed and bread and soup.

I explain to my daughter, "As a society, we've decided we're okay with giving people food and shelter, but we require them to commit a crime first."

And this is true. We still do it. We arrest people for not having a home, and I'm good with this if it's done right. Have a special jail for them. Don't put 'em in regular jail with people who've been violent, or smoked pot. Don't get me wrong, I'm not suggesting we go easy on these homeless criminals. I want their jail to have all the regular jail stuff, like beds, food, and maybe even a library. And then maybe let's give them keys to the jail, and make it house-shaped. Let's get tough on crime!

I sometimes teach comedy classes to "housing insecure youth." There are some very funny young folks living on the streets or in shelters who have something to say. I was heading into the community center-type building where the classes take place and I overheard the most amazing conversation. A young woman was being asked to prove that she was homeless enough to receive services. They can't have people faking it to get these great, high-demand services I'm guessing. I mean, free comedy classes from Keith Lowell Jensen! Grab me my dirty clothes, I've got a scam to pull!

How the hell do you prove that you're homeless? There were homes across the street from the place. I guess they could have just started knocking on doors and asked if she lived there.

And if someone said yes, well that solved the problem anyway, win/win.

To be fair, the person asking for the proof wasn't being an asshole. These requirements are put on them by keepers of the state's purse. The social worker with the clipboard tried to be helpful.

"If you sleep in a car in front of a liquor store, you can have the person working at the liquor store sign that you stay in a car."

Um... I'm pretty sure the person in the liquor store will call that special number, the one the boss told them to call if someone is sleeping in a car in front of the liquor store. After all, it is illegal to be homeless, and in what other circumstances are we asked to prove we're committing a crime that we confess to and seek help for?

"Yeah, I'm a kleptomaniac and I'd like help."

Can you prove you're a kleptomaniac?

"Well, this is your iPhone right? Sign here please."

"I am a drug addict, and I'd like to get clean."

Can you PROVE you're a drug addict?

"Sure. What do you have that I can smoke, snort, or shoot?"

There is also the question of who is this person that makes this necessary? Is there someone who lives indoors trying to get that good homeless shit? Is someone sitting in their climate-controlled living room, watching a big old TV, and seeing a soup kitchen on the news thinks, "I bet them homeless bastards get the good soup! I'm tired of eating this Progresso bullshit. They got that gourmet, organic Wolfgang Puck Organic Free Range Chicken Noodle."

I don't know if a guy like this is really out there, waiting to cheat the system out of a free bowl of soup, and a comedy class, but I don't mind having him in my class, as long as he doesn't heckle, or do prop comedy.

I once needed some free medical attention for chronic sinus infections. I spent eight hours in a crowded hot waiting room waiting for them to prove I was poor enough to qualify. The free clinic reminds me of the slobby straight dude who is worried all gay men are attracted to them. Look, cargo shorts and sandals, you ain't all that. Now relax and give me some penicillin.

The next time I needed medical attention it was for a swollen red spot on my eye, I skipped the free clinic and got advice from the nice Mexican lady who worked at Bag of Bagels. I didn't have to prove to her that I was poor. I just had to buy a bagel, and she told me to put olive oil on the spider bite. It worked.

Charlie Chaplin stole food. Charlie Chaplin went to Jail. My daughter and I had several good teachable moments. Then Charlie accidentally puts cocaine in his soup until he's wired to the gills, which he makes look like a pretty good time.

"What is that white powder, daddy?" my little girl asks.

"Um… it's salt, baby. Charlie really likes salt. Why don't we go play outside for a while?"

THE BREAK-IN

The last time I called the cops was when my home was broken into and my car stolen. I'd already made the decision not to call them again. I'd gone from thinking that they'd damn well better serve us when we need 'em, given how much they harass and bully us, and yeah, some of us much more than others, to realizing that even when you needed the service they were supposed to offer, they either did nothing or they made things worse. But on this occasion, stressed as I was at having someone in my house while my kid was there sleeping, and also needing my car back, and at my wife's insistence, I called them.

The thief had come in through a window after jumping the wall into the backyard of the duplex we were renting half of. They did a quick sweep through the place, grabbing my laptop and my wife's purse with her car keys. They made their getaway in our 10-year-old Toyota Corolla.

The cops showed up, and the first thing they asked me was if I had enemies. The question made me laugh. I was pretty sure this was simply a financially motivated crime of opportunity, but yeah, sure, I have enemies.

"I'm a comedian with a really big mouth who posts constantly on social media. My list of enemies is epic."

"Well, what kind of stuff do you post?"

The truth was, I posted a lot of anti-cop stuff but I decided now wasn't the time to share this. "Um, I'm very political. I don't think this was done by anyone who knew me. They'd have known to grab the records and comic books."

"Yeah, okay," he said, and I got the sense that he was worried I was gonna start telling him about my records and comic books.

I was glad it was an Asian, and a Hispanic cop. I thought about asking them if they could rough me up a little, so the neighbors weren't suspicious of me having cops over for a friendly visit. They did what cops do when poor people get robbed, nothing. If you want help don't call the cops, call your mom. I called mine and she came and took my daughter to school.

My wife read online that most cars are recovered within a few miles of where they were taken so, after borrowing Mom's van to pick my daughter back up from school, and giving said daughter some fast-food French fries (a most rare treat in our household) to buy her tolerance, she started driving around our neighborhood slowly getting further from our house.

She called me, "I'm in your mom's van parked behind our car."

"WHAT? The cops found it?"

"No. I found it!" She gave me the cross streets and I got a ride to go grab our car.

"We're not touching it until the cops get here," she instructed, with a tone to her voice that told me this wouldn't be an argument I'd be winning.

I really wanted to jump in and drive away, but she was the badass who found it, so she'd be the one to call the shots. As we waited a big truck pulled up front bumper to front bumper with our Corolla. The driver went into a nearby house. A minute later he came back out, looked at us, and left. The cop showed up, and she invited me to start the car. The battery was dead. As we talked to the cop a man and a woman came out of that same house the truck driver had visited and glared at us.

The cop asked me, "Is this yours?"

The child car seats were missing from the back seat, but in their place was a huge television.

"Nope," I answered, blowing it. "But can I have it? I mean, for my trouble?"

"No. It's evidence," she answered.

"If nobody claims it can I have it?"

"No." She lifted the TV from our car, and put it in the trunk of her squad car.

As she did so I looked over at the couple who were still glaring at us, even harder now, and I smiled. The picture had come into pretty sharp focus. They were using our car to take this TV somewhere, but the battery was dead. The dude in the truck came to give 'em up a jump, but they had noticed my wife watching the car by then, so he took off.

And now, they watched us loading the TV into the squad car, and I wished I could say to them, "You'd think you, you of all people, would know better than to leave anything of value in the car."

I didn't sleep very well for a few months after the break-in, but I also felt like we'd been a real pain in the ass, taking our car back when they were in the middle of using it, and I hoped that might discourage them from wanting to work with us again.

I have to ask myself if it was worth calling the police. They didn't manage to nab anyone, and it felt like they didn't really try which was frustrating, but I have to also be thankful that they didn't come up with a suspect who then ended up dead, or in a cycle of repeat imprisonments. It really was a huge violation that impacted our sense of security but playing any part in such a broken system wasn't going to help us sleep any better.

Obviously, I hope never to be in the position to have to decide on calling the cops or not but if it did happen again, I don't think I'd bother getting them involved. After all my wife is the person who cracked the case, found the car, and ordered us an alarm system.

The cops did nothing for us, and they took my TV.

MICHAEL

"Look at my beautiful country! I want you to know how beautiful my country is." Lena was a precocious eight-year-old who sat next to me on the bus to Belize City, Belize.

I'd already been on the bus for an hour, having started out in Chetumal, Mexico. Her mother and little sister took the two open seats behind me. She plopped down next to me and started talking. This was before I had a little extrovert kid of my own and I delighted in listening to her serve as the best ambassador Belize could hope for.

When the family reached their stop, Lena said goodbye, and my friend Steve who I'd been traveling with took the seat next to me, but only for a minute. "Dude, you always end up talking to people. I'm going to go meet someone and talk to 'em."

He pushed himself, getting up and taking a new seat in the back of the bus where he met Tony; Tony who had a duffle bag full of marijuana that he grew in the rainforest. "Hey Keith, come back here. I met someone."

As we sat chatting and laughing with Tony two Young men in uniforms boarded the bus. I wasn't sure if they were police, military, or some weird combination of the two. I was in my mid-twenties, and they looked considerably younger than me. They began searching some of the passengers.

Both of them carried machine guns with their fingers resting on the triggers. I had to move my head as one of these kid cops chatted with the man sitting across the aisle from me, paying no attention to his gun which was pointed at my face as we bounced down the bumpy road.

Tony didn't seem worried. He explained after the cops got off the bus that they didn't care about him, they were looking for guns coming up from Guatemala. He asked us where we were heading and when we said, "Belize City," he told us this was a mistake.

"Belize City is a dump. You guys come out to Caye Caulker with me. It's beautiful."

And so we followed a stranger with a giant bag of weed to a small Central American island we'd never heard of because Steve wanted to be better at making friends.

We climbed into a boat that to me seemed more suited for racing than taxiing. As I put on a life jacket I noticed that I was the only person on the boat wearing one. Families, including young children, looked bored as I held on for dear life and we rocketed away from Belize City toward Caye Caulker.

Tony steered us right. The island was beautiful. He led us to a hostel, which was just a house with bunk beds in a couple of the bedrooms. We were told it was five Belizean a night, (about $2.50 American) to sleep indoors, but we could pitch our hammocks in the yard for two Belizean. We went the cheap route as much for the sense of adventure as for thrift.

We were pleased to find out a group of locals all hung out and made dinner together in this yard every night. Steve and I got a shopping list from them, so we could contribute, and we walked over to the tiny grocery store. This was a slice of paradise. Fish, just plucked from the ocean, were on the grill. I kept to my veganism by shoveling perfect avocados into my mouth with chips and salsa, and various fruits. I struck up a conversation with a friendly, easy-going local named Michael. Tony rolled joints and took in some money as he passed them around.

Steve and I were giddy as we settled into our hammock later to try and get some sleep.

"Good job striking up a conversation, man. You kind of hit the jackpot," I praised him.

The next day we went snorkeling with Jean, a tour guide Tony had introduced as to. He made us dinner on a tiny island. We saw nurse sharks and rays and tropical reefs and all around had one of the best days imaginable. After sharing a beer with Jean back on Caye Caulker, we walked back to the hostel and the BBQ. Michael pulled up in a golf cart. As he got out of his cart and walked toward us everyone got quiet. Two joints that were making their way around the circle were suddenly dropped, and stepped on.

"Hey gang, what's up. Where's the party?" Michael asked.

Steve and I had no idea what was happening but we caught the silence and tense vibe so we kept quiet as well.

"No party tonight, Michael," Tony answered him.

"Ah, no?" he asked in an annoyed tone.

"No," Tony replied, bluntly.

And Michael drove off.

"How come we don't like Michael now?" I asked.

The man next to me answered, "Michael is the cop tonight. I was the cop last night."

"What do you mean he's the cop tonight?"

"We only have one police officer on duty on the island at a time. Right now it's Michael. If he sees you smoking pot he'll take you to jail."

Tony laughed. "Tell him where the jail is."

"It's in Michael's house when he's the cop. It's in my house when I'm the cop."

"Wait, what now?" I was blown away. "If Michael saw us smoking pot we'd have to go hang out at his house all night?"

"Yeah, that's right," and everyone had a good laugh at our baffled disbelieving expressions.

The next morning, after saying goodbye to Tony and to Caye Caulker we hitchhiked and bussed our way to San Ignacio, a small town near the Belize Guatemala border. There we met an American who ran a bakery. He explained that Belize accepted American foreign aid but with the aid came American drug laws, and overnight an illegal drug market, and gangs. A group of young men walked past us and one of them snatched Steve's blue bandana off his head.

"What the fuck?" Steve snapped as he grabbed it back.

"No blue, man. Only red, for love." We stared at each other for a tense minute before they continued on their way and we on ours.

We made our way back to Mexico where we hitched a ride from a semi driver delivering a load to the city of Merida. As with most of the rides we caught, the driver wanted to practice speaking English.

"How do you say police?" he asked, having to yell as his old truck bounced all over the place on a decrepit two-lane highway.

"You got it. Police!" I yelled back.

"No, no, what do YOU call them? When you don't like them."

"Oh! I see what you mean. Yeah, we call 'em pigs."

"Pigs? Like..." And he pushed his nose up and made oink sounds.

"Ha. Yeah, pigs."

He laughed hard at this. "Pigs! I like this. They are pigs, perfect."

"Well, what do you call them?"

"Perro."

I didn't recognize the word. "Perro?"

"Uh, yes, perro, you know... um, like this." and he pulled out his wallet, bit it, and growled.

I was in a stranger's semi-truck as it bounced and rattled with a deafening noise down a poorly maintained highway somewhere in Mexico, the driver biting his wallet and growling. His perro impersonation got more and more intense and I was laughing too hard to tell him I got it.

"Dog!" I finally managed to shout through the guffaws.

"YES! YES! It's dog. They are dogs. They take a bite out of our wallets like dogs."

We laughed together and continued trading English and Spanish words, now friends after bonding over a shared dislike of cops. Some things go beyond borders, truly.

HI PIGS

I was deep, lost, crazy in love with a girl who was traveling in Europe with another guy, no, not just another guy, a guy who stayed up all night reading philosophy, a guy who played bass for a hip and successful band, a guy who seemed to effortlessly embrace and embody the intellectual and artistic identity that I chased without ever quite catching up to. So, I asked my friend Nicole's girlfriend Terry out for a bike ride.

Terry was a lesbian, but she was oddly flirty with me and when I asked her to go for a ride along the American River she was quick to say yes, enthusiastic even. Most of my lesbian friends had at least tried messing around with a guy at some point in their lives. I was hoping maybe I could be that guy to Terry even if just to confirm to herself that she really wasn't into guys. I felt low enough at that point, self-esteem-wise, that this seemed a good use of my powers.

These were the thoughts of a scoundrel. Beyond being unrealistic, I was showing no respect for Terry or Nicole, and on some level I knew it, but rather than just calling the date off, or going on the date and letting it be the innocent bike ride I'm sure Terry meant it to be, I opted to just flake. I loaded my VW Bus up with friends and we drove to Reno,

Nevada, a dirty little town that boasted the closest legal gambling to Sacramento, California.

We had no interest in gambling which is good as none of us were 21 or in possession of disposable income but the neon gaudiness of this dirty town seemed a suitable backdrop for a drunken adventure.

The sun was on the horizon as we pulled into town. We saw a group of folks around our age skateboarding in a deserted parking lot. To our surprise and dismay, they were not friendly. This broke all the rules. They had skateboards. We had skateboards. They were supposed to be friendly. We put our boards back in the bus and popped open a few bottles of wine.

Once the sun finished making its departure, allowing the full effect of the kitchy, vintage neon signs to take effect we began our stumble through town. Tourists avoided us or stared at us in disgust in just the way we wanted. We were their idea of scumbags. I knew real scumbags I'd have loved to have introduced them to, but it was fun to pretend I was something more than a make-believe wretch, playing drunken poet for an evening, like the accountants and lawyers who put on leather jackets to cosplay being bikers on weekends. I composed singalongs and we had a jolly time.

Crossing a wide street I looked up and realized I was in the gaze of two Reno cops.

"Hi, pigs!" I said, with as friendly a voice as I could conjure.

With the wine warming my cheeks I wager it was pretty friendly.

The cop in the passenger seat answered, "Hi," back, sounding quite friendly himself.

The driver turned on the siren, and pulled to the curb. "Hey, you, with the mouth," he barked at me as he stepped out of the squad car. "Why did you say that?"

"Hi?" I asked.

"Why did you call us pigs, smartass?"

"I don't know. Why are you calling me smartass?"

"Because you're being a smartass."

"Well, you're being pigs."

"You feel like spending the night in jail, do ya?"

"For calling you pigs? Your partner didn't mind. You guys even call yourselves that in the Pig Bowl every year. Why do you have to make a big deal out of it."

He was getting redder and redder each time I spoke. "Kid, you're in Nevada."

Something about me had made it clear to him that I was from out of state. "There's no such thing as a decriminalized offense in Nevada. Do you know what that means?"

"I surely do not," I answered honestly.

"Well, it means I can take you to jail for any offense. I can take you to jail for jaywalking for instance."

"I wasn't jaywalking. I wouldn't have been in front of your vehicle if you hadn't been stopped at a red light, which gives me the green light," I answered honestly.

I was starting to lose my wine buzz.

"Is that what you saw?" he asked his partner, who didn't mind being called a pig.

"Nope. I saw some jaywalking," answered the pig.

"Look here, asshole," the cop whispered loudly, as he leaned into me. "We were happy to let you idiots wander around having your fun. You didn't need to attract our attention but you did. You begged us to interact with you. So here it is. Why did you do that? Now I'll ask again, do you want to spend the night in jail?"

"No," I answered honestly. "Jesus, man, I'm just drunk. It seemed funny, and it was friendly enough. I don't understand why you gotta make such a fuss about it. Can ya just get called a pig once in a while? Isn't that the trade-off to the bootlickers who call you a hero the rest of the time?"

"Here's the deal, punk. Reno is my town. If I see you again in my town, I'm taking you to jail. So I suggest you get the hell out of my town right now. In fact, I suggest you get out of my state."

"Well, that would be my pleasure. May I go?"

"Yes. Get out of my face."

They got in their car, and we walked toward my bus, and as they pulled away from the curb I called back, "Bye, pigs."

I knew by the immediate flaring of the brake lights that he heard me and we started running.

"Why do you always have to be such an asshole?" my friend, Bill, asked.

"I don't know," I answered, honestly.

MY HEROES OF CRIME: NICK

From Robin Hood, to Bonnie and Clyde, to The Usual Suspects, to Ice T or KRS-1's tales of crime and running from the law, there's something about a noble criminal that I've always adored. There are a few real-life criminals who have impressed me when I've had the pleasure of witnessing their lawlessness firsthand, and one of the most impressive was a magical idiot named Nick.

"Hey, Erick, why do you hate that Nick guy so much?" I asked my older brother one summer night as we sat on his porch drinking 40oz bottles of malt liquor.

"Lots of reasons. He's just a dick." I could see Erick trying to recall a specific example to summarize Nick's dick-ishness. "He's one of those guys where anytime you ask him where something is, he answers, 'If it was in your ass you'd know.'"

Maybe it was the malt liquor's fault, but this struck me as the funniest thing I'd ever heard, and I started laughing. Erick's disgust with my laughter triggered more laughing. He went to bed and left me to my guffaws.

I was crashing on Erick's couch while between gigs. Most evenings after he arrived home from a day of construction work we'd sit on the front porch and drink too much beer. During the day I'd write, or find excuses and distractions and not write. When my sister-in-law Robin invited me to run some errands with her I was glad to get out of the house. Our first stop was Mervyn's, the ubiquitous department store that started in the 60s, but didn't manage to survive the nineties. Mervyns was cooler than Wal-Mart, less cool than Target. Robin elbowed me to get my attention.

"Hey, watch this," she nodded in the direction of Nick who had just entered the department store empty-handed.

Nick was good-looking in a haggard, damaged kind of way. He headed straight toward the customer service counter, reaching out and grabbing a couple of pairs of jeans off a pile as he passed by. He returned the jeans. With no receipt, he could only get store credit. He was very polite and understanding, and laughed with the woman handling the returns at the ridiculousness of his own girlfriend not knowing his size. The clerk decided she'd give him cash back, just this one time. He thanked her profusely.

As Nick walked back out of the store with cash in hand I stood amazed. He'd figured out the Matrix. He was as close to a Jedi Knight as I'd ever seen in real life. And to this day, if you ask me where something is, I'm likely to point out the undeniable fact that if it was in your butt, you'd know.

SOMETIMES I'M THE COP

James owned and manned the counter at Decades Costumes on Del Paso Blvd. A half-century or more ago The Boulevard was a destination for Sacramentans wanting a night out, boasting an ice-skating rink, movie theaters, and restaurants. It was now a rundown neglected street with liquor stores, storefront churches, funky art galleries denying their role in gentrification, and one high-end furniture store blatantly betting on gentrification. The city has promised/threatened to invest in the boulevard and restore it to its former glory for years but here it remained a neglected treasure trove of slightly seedy local-owned businesses in vintage architecture and Lil' Joe's, home of the $2 steak.

James wasn't holding his breath for this restoration. He had a densely packed costume shop that the local theater folks knew about, as did the more savvy second-hand shoppers. He was content with a leisurely schedule most days of watching the regular characters who lived and panhandled and tended to what James referred to as "other business" in front of his shop. He'd enjoy the daily soap opera while filling up his utility sink with the cans of Natty Light that he steadily emptied throughout the day.

I loved Decades Costumes and James. When I was in a

sketch comedy troupe he was always willing to rent us costumes for what we could afford, even when what we could afford was nothing. He'd send us out the door with a promise to thank him at the end of our show and to put a mention of his "promotional consideration" in our playbill. I feel like I still owe him so much, so I'm inclined to continue plugging Decades Costumes, even though he closed shop for good years ago. Perhaps you can visit them in your dreams. James would like that.

Back in the early 90s I was struggling to come up with a Halloween costume that would sufficiently blow minds. Then it hit me; cop! A cop was far and above the scariest thing that you could see entering your Halloween party. I headed to Decades.

"Hey James, can you rent me a cop outfit?"

"No. Absolutely not," he answered, dropping the enthusiasm with which he'd greeted me and going back to the fashion magazine he was reading, taking a sip of Natty Lite through a plastic straw.

"Ha. What? Why not?"

"What do you want the costume for?"

"Halloween."

"No, no, no. It's illegal to walk around dressed as a cop, and it's illegal for me to help you. You'll get us both in trouble."

"Oh. Um… it's for a show."

"Keith…"

"What?!"

"You just said it's for Halloween."

"Yeah, a Halloween show."

"Okay. Where's the show?"

"It's at my friend Todd's house."

"No," he answered again as he got up and walked through the sparkly beaded curtain that separated the front of the shop from the back.

I heard the empty beer can hit the other empties that

were already in the sink. James minced back through the beads popping open a fresh can.

"C'mon, James! I won't tell anyone I got it from you."

"Okay, I'm gonna rent you a security guard outfit, and you're gonna promise me in writing on your rental contract that it is ONLY to be worn onstage."

"Yes!"

And with that, James turned back into the wacky guy who loved to play dress-up. We went through the uniform shirts, fake badges, hats, and holster belts, intentionally choosing different colors than those of our local PD. James started to get excited seeing me turn into a cop.

"Oh my God, you need a mustache! And glasses!" He pulled out a selection of real human hair mustaches.

I tried not to think too hard on the potential hair farms that give us real human hair mustaches as James used spirit gum to stick a full, blonde 'stache to my upper lip. I looked in the mirror and immediately got the giggles at the douchey-looking police officer looking back at me.

"Do you know why I pulled you over?" I asked, lowering my glasses.

"Yuck! Oh my God, you're too good at this. Take it off. You're creeping me out."

I paid James, after getting the broke friend discount, and despite all the promises he made me give, and sign, about wearing the outfit in public, he let me walk out his front door as Officer Jensen. Back in Midtown, I made my way to Greta's Cafe to freak out Bryna, a woman I was forever crushing on, and sometimes kissing on. As I crossed the railroad tracks I saw two kids walking on the tracks toward me. I decided to test out my costume.

"Excuse me. Just what do you think you're doing?" I snapped.

They looked up in shock. They were the most darling, innocent-looking siblings, and I don't think they were used to being spoken to sharply by authority figures.

"W… w… what?" blinked the boy, who looked to be about twelve, a year or two older than his sister.

"We're just walking on the tracks?" little sis answered.

"Just walking on the tracks? You're just WALKING ON the TRACKS, are you?"

"Is that against the law?" big brother asked.

"Well, that depends. Are you a train? I mean, you don't look like a train. And these are called train tracks now aren't they? Over here, where I'm walking, this is called a side-walk. Can you see the difference, side-WALK, and TRAIN TRACKS? I don't think it's that complicated."

"We won't walk on them anymore," he replied.

"We promise," she answered.

"Yes, well, that may not be good enough," I said, pulling out a small pad that James had equipped me with, and a pen.

I looked up and saw their scared faces. I hadn't meant to really upset them. It hadn't occurred to me that I could actually look that much like a cop. Feeling suddenly guilty I put the pad and pen away.

Leaning forward, in a soft voice I told them, "Hey, I'm sorry. I'm just kidding. You guys are young and it's a beautiful day. You have fun. And listen, you live your life, and love each other, and everyone, every day, okay?"

They both stared at me, baffled. I said, "Okay?"

"Okay," they answered in unison.

"GREAT!" I shouted back, skipping flamboyantly away from them down the sidewalk, singing tra-la-la, and making sure they'd remember this run-in with a loony cop for the rest of their days.

At Greta's, I stood at the counter and stared intensely at Bryna. She noticed and so turned and stared back at me with a defiant look on her face. God, I loved this woman. I pointed at her and made the "come here" motion with my finger. I couldn't believe she didn't recognize me.

When she reached the counter I said, "Do you wanna make out?"

I thought surely my voice would give me away. She stared, confused. She knew something was up, but still wasn't sure what. I pulled down my mirrored glasses.

"Oh my God! Get the fuck out of here. Go!" she commanded.

"But I want to order a coffee!" I laughed.

"No. You leave. No coffee," she said and walked away shaking her head.

When she got back to whatever food prep she'd been working on she looked back at me one more time, smiled in spite of herself, and went back to shaking her head. I am a charmer. Is it any wonder it only took another twenty years before she agreed to marry me?

TRAFFIC STOPS

The life of a stand-up comedian is 90% driving. Luckily I love driving, whether it's with a car full of comedians tagging each other's jokes, or on my own with my music blasting.

I got up one warm summer morning, grabbed a coffee from the corner shop, hopped into a rental car, and hit the road, proud of myself for starting out so early toward my gig at a Native American gaming casino. I'd reach the high desert in Oregon early enough to eat a free lunch and check into my room for a nap, and hit the stage refreshed and recharged.

I set the cruise control to keep me just 7 miles over the speed limit, figuring I wasn't likely to get pulled over for that. Without cruise control, it was just too easy to slip into speeding as I sang along, loudly, to my music on the long stretches of I-5 that feel like a low budget animation background just looping by again and again.

I looked to my left and saw Harris Ranch.

"Ha, I didn't know they had a Harris Ranch up here." I thought. "They don't. You're an idiot."

I also thought, realizing that I got on the freeway going south instead of north and had now driven almost three hours in the wrong direction. I got off the southbound freeway in a panic, got on the northbound freeway in a panic, and took off the cruise control, driving way over my 7-miles-an-hour-past-the-speed-limit safe speed, in a panic.

I did the math in my head, I'd left myself enough grace that, if luck held up, I'd still manage to get there just before showtime. No stops for fast food, and hopefully, the gas tank would hold out.

I was almost to the California/Oregon border when my phone rang. It was David Tribble, the booker who sent comics on these crazy one-nighter runs all over the western states, what we comedians referred to as Tribble Runs.

"Hey, David. How are you?"

"Just calling to check that you're on your way."

"Oh yeah man. I've been on the road awhile."

"Where are you?"

"I crossed into Oregon about an hour ago," I lied.

"An hour ago? Cutting it close, aren't you?"

I hadn't lied by a large enough margin.

"Well there was some traffic," I lied again.

"I've been watching. I didn't see any traffic on the 5. You're on the 5 yeah?"

"Well, I don't know why you didn't see any. Guess it didn't get reported. But I hit it. I'm good though. I've never been late for a gig you've booked me for. I won't be late to this one."

"I don't like cutting it close. You never know what can happen. Car trouble, actual traffic, whatever."

I heard "the *actual* traffic" the way it was intended. He knew I lied, I knew I lied, we both knew that we both knew that I lied. Then the police lights flashed on behind me. Damn it!

"Hey David, I gotta jump off. I don't have hands free, and I don't want a ticket," I said.

This wasn't quite a lie. I didn't want a ticket.

I hung up and pulled over, quickly scanning the area, my brain racing. Getting out of a ticket was an art form I had not mastered, but I was eager to do so. There was the cop in

Riverside, who caught me racing to the college as there was an already seated audience waiting to watch the film reels I was transporting for Spike and Mike's Festival of Animation.

He was impressed, as he was a fan of the animation festival I was working for.

"I love Spike and Mike," he said, giving me hope.

"I'll write the ticket real fast and get you on your way." he finished, dashing all hope.

He made good on this and then had the nerve to ask me if he could get free tickets to the fest.

"Fuck no!" I told him, before driving off in a huff.

Then there was the last time an Oregon cop had me pulled over when I used a broken yellow line to pass a truck, and the guy coming at me swerved even though he was a million miles away.

When the cop asked if I knew why he pulled me over I took a chance at cracking a joke and said, "Because that other driver was such a pussy?"

He was not amused. I got a ticket.

But there was also the cop later that same day who pulled me over for veering into the other line while admiring an amazing view. My eyes teared up as I told him I was actually being safe. Using the other lane, after checking that it was clear for miles and miles, so I could safely get a quick peek at the gorgeous landscape, and that one more ticket would mean this trip was actually non-profitable and I just couldn't afford to throw away a whole weekend and not bring home any money, and to my surprise he actually let me go.

The game was on. The cop approached my window. "Was I speeding, officer? I didn't think I was going over 70."

"You just crossed into Oregon. The speed limit here is 55. You were also on your phone."

"Yeah, I was calling 911 to report the fire," I lied.

I'd notice a small fire burning on the hillside I'd passed just minutes earlier. It was a good day for lying. I was glad Tribble had helped me stretch and ready my lying muscles.

"You can check my phone," I bluffed.

"I don't need to check your phone," he replied. "What brings you to Oregon?"

"Well, that's actually none of your fuckin' business," I didn't say because I didn't have time to go to jail.

"I'm a comedian. I have a gig at an Indian gaming casino and I'm cutting it close."

"How long have you been a comedian?" he asked.

"Why? Are we taping a fucking podcast? Is this the time for a friendly chat? Should we grab a cup of coffee and get to know each other better?" I didn't say because I really didn't have time to go to jail.

"A few years," I answered, hoping he wasn't gonna ask me to tell him a joke.

He ran my license, looked at my insurance, and didn't ask me to tell him a joke and he didn't give me a ticket. "Okay. Watch your speed and if you need to make a call, pull over. You can go."

I pulled out, a little insulted that he didn't ask me to tell him a joke.

I made the gig on time, with the gas gauge pointing to E. I performed for three young Native American men who worked at the casino, and one couple who were making out in a booth in the back of the room.

ROCKLIN COPS

I lived for a bit with my parents in Rocklin, California, where the cops were notoriously obnoxious. I was riding shotgun in a car with my brother Edward behind the wheel and our friends Bill and Mike in the back seat, when a cop pulled us over for having long hair. Mike, who was 15-years-old, stomped his cigarette out as soon as the lights and sirens came on behind us. He was worried he'd get in trouble for smoking.

The Rocklin cop approached the window agitated. "Step out of the car please, all of you, with your hands where we can see them."

He and his partner both had their hands on their guns though they still had them holstered. We slowly got out of the car.

"What were you hiding?" the Rocklin cop asked Mike.

Mike sounded like he might cry. "What? I wasn't hiding anything."

"I turned on my lights, and you immediately bent down."

"No I didn't!"

"You did. Why did you bend forward?"

This was as much interrogation as Mike could take. He spilled the beans, and gave up the whole caper. "I was putting out a cigarette. I was afraid I'd get in trouble for smoking."

"What kind of cigarette?" the Rocklin cop asked, digging further into the crime of the century.

"What kind? Marlboro," Mike answered, not understanding the question.

"Tobacco," my brother answered for him. "Just tobacco."

"I'M NOT TALKING TO YOU RIGHT NOW, CHIEF!" the Rocklin cop barked at my brother.

He went to the car and he found Mike's cigarette stamped out on a smashed Coke can.

"Why is your car such a mess?" he asked Edward, getting a shrug in reply.

"What is this?" the Rocklin cop asked, pulling out an ominous-looking lump of matter.

I *think* it used to be a hamburger," Edward answered.

The Rocklin cop threw it down in disgust, glaring at my brother. He started sliding his hand up behind the dashboard. Then the Rocklin cop spotted the piece of evidence he'd been looking for.

"And what is this?" he asked, pointing to a pile of white powder on the floor of the back section of the car.

"Laundry detergent," answered Edward, truthfully.

The white powder didn't look like anything other than laundry detergent. Nobody who'd seen illicit substances that come in powdered form would have mistaken this white clumpy powder with blue crystals for anything but laundry detergent. The cop licked his finger and stuck it in the powder.

He smelled it. He prepared to taste it.

"Hey, you really don't want to taste that. It's soap, for reals." Edward's warning had the opposite of its intended effect.

The Rocklin cop smiled, sure that my brother was actually concerned that he was about to be busted. He took a taste and immediately started spitting, but seemed to have trouble working up enough saliva. He rushed to his squad car to find something to rinse his mouth out. And we started laughing.

The other Rocklin cop yelled, "Be quiet! Stop laughing!" but he had trouble getting it out because he was laughing.

Even little Mike was no longer afraid. The Rocklin cop focused in on him, grabbing him by the arm and putting him up against the car to pat him down.

"Nice hair. Are you a boy or a girl?" the cop asked him as he ran his hands over Mike.

"The way you're going, you're about to find out," Mike answered.

We all started laughing again.

It just seemed so surreal, to be in the late 80s and having some small-town cop harass us for long hair, like we'd stepped back through time and were making our way to Woodstock, or to San Francisco for the summer of love.

Rocklin Cop let Edward know that his cracked mirror, loose bumper, and broken taillight meant he was one infraction short of reckless driving and could go to jail, "...and what do you think of that?"

Edward politely told him he'd rather not go to jail, and yes, sir, and thank you sir, and eventually we drove off with a few fix-it tickets shoved in the glove box. Edward slid his hands under the dashboard, just as the cop had when he'd been searching the car. My brother's contraband, which would've gotten him a lot more than fix-it tickets, was about two inches past where the Rocklin cop had stopped his search as he was distracted by the laundry soap.

DALE THE NARC

During freshman year, at Roseville High, I walked into class one day to see this thirty-year-old-looking dude sitting at a desk with a backpack. This was Dale. I couldn't believe they were trying to pass this guy off as a student. He needed a shave. And the punchline came a week or two later when they gave up, and he transitioned into just the campus cop. You'd think they'd transfer him somewhere and bring in a different cop, but no, they just owned it.

Yeah, ha ha, we tried to trick you. Seriously though, you will respect my authority.

Even when he was clearly the school cop he was plain clothes, and by plain clothes I mean he dressed like an adult's idea of what a teenager dressed like in 1987, with ripped jeans, converse, and a flannel shirt open over a printed t-shirt. Thankfully they didn't go as far as the backward baseball cap. I have no idea if he was actually law enforcement, but we students considered him a pig all the same.

Most of my interactions with Dale came when a group of bad kids enlisted me to be their lookout so that they could smoke during lunch break. It was a frustrating period for me, when I was failing to make any friends. I accepted this demeaning position because it beat sitting alone in the cafeteria.

"Hi Dale!" I'd shout if I saw him heading our way, and cigarettes were quickly stomped out.

On another occasion I was ditching one of my classes, playing video games across the street at the gas station/convenience store and suddenly he was next to me. "Hey dude, getting the high score?"

"What? Oh, nah man, but this is further than I've ever gotten."

"Cool. You know I gotta tell you to go back to school, right?"

"Yeah, that makes sense. Can I finish this game?"

"Sure."

"Damn, never mind. I just died."

"All out of quarters?"

"Yeah."

"I got ya," and Dale dropped a quarter in before the "Continue" countdown expired.

I guess he was all right in a dorky guy too old to be wearing ripped jeans kinda way.

KRYPTONITE DONG

Dude was having one hell of a morning after. He was fast asleep sitting behind the wheel of his illegally parked four-door boat of a car, driver seat reclined, his pants around his ankles, his underwear on the moon as far as I could tell, and his flaccid penis basking in the morning sun.

I was on a waiting list for breakfast at a local restaurant and I appreciated the entertainment as I stood laughing with the rest of the hungry crowd lined up on the busy sidewalk. A black and white squad car pulled up behind dude's car and two cops, one male, one female, got out, hanging their nightsticks on their belts. The male cop strutted up to dude's window while his partner waited by the squad car.

The cop peaked in the car, and upon seeing penis exclaimed loudly, "What the fuck? What the fuck?" and quickly backed away.

We all started laughing. His partner asked what was going on.

"He's got his pants down! His Goddamned dork is out," he answered, sounding honestly horrified and even a bit nauseated.

We all laughed harder. The female cop walked up to the window and knocked on it with her nightstick. Dude looked up. She did the universal hand movement for 'Roll down your window.'

Dude rolled down his window. "Sir, pull your pants up."

"Wha? Oh, shit, sorry," dude pulled his pants up.

At this point, with the exposed penis put away, the male cop was like Superman recovering after being exposed to kryptonite. His partner had gotten some denim pulled up over that kryptonite and he was a superhero once again. He went and arrested the now-clothed drunk. His partner's smile and expression of bemusement made my day as I imagined their relationship was forever changed.

MARI'S NEW CAR

Mari was a punk rocker. She chopped her own hair to short uneven lengths, and sported the requisite leather jacket and boots of an early 90s punk. Catherine was delightfully nerdy, with glasses, mid-length curly hair worn in a bun, an expansive collection of sweaters, and an encyclopedic knowledge of The Pogues.

Mari bought Catherine's car. I was in the backseat of the car with my friends Christian and Ryan as it was barreling toward Santa Cruz when a handshake deal was reached by the two women sitting on opposite sides of the vinyl front bench seats. Catherine was driving, Mari immediately began modifying the car to make it her own. She reached up and tore the ceiling liner. We three drunk boys in the back followed her lead.

Over the next two days there was jumping on the hood, and kicking the doors shut, and otherwise being so darn punk rock with this long four door automobile (I never know what make, model and year car I'm in. It was from the 70s and big). It never occurred to us as we trashed the car that such wasteful, conspicuous consumption, a suburban kid's idea of being so darn punk rock, wasn't exactly sticking it to the man. If we were sticking it to anyone it was Catherine who fretted, and reminded Mari repeatedly that no money had changed hands yet. She thought that perhaps we could wait until she'd been paid to thrash the car, but Mari assured her a handshake was as good as a check.

By that night Catherine was a wreck. She, our sober driver, now had four very drunk punks in her increasingly beaten and battered car. We'd been awful enough before the alcohol was added. We now turned the obnoxiousness all the way up. She drove along the pacific ocean looking for a place to camp out for at least a few hours of sleep before starting the four-hour drive back to Sacramento. Her slow speed, and frequent braking brought the flashing red and blue lights. We were being pulled over.

Catherine tried talking to the cop, her voice shaky, her forehead dotted with beads of sweat. The cop walked back to her squad car with Catherine's license, to run it through her dashboard computer.

Christian got out of the car. "Sir, get back in the car!"

"I just want to talk to you, officer."

"Get Back In The Car! NOW!" she ordered, her hand now on her gun.

Christian got back in the car.

As the cop made her way back toward the driver-side window, I rolled down my own window, and politely said, "Officer, can I talk to you?"

And oddly enough, she said, "Yes. Please step out of the car."

I walked to the rear of the car, drunk as could be. "Officer, the driver is sober, but she's a wreck. Look at her? She's a nice kid who somehow ended up with a bunch of drunk punks in her car and she just wants to get this night over with so she can never make the mistake of hanging out with this crew again."

"Has she been drinking?"

"Not a drop. The rest of us, yes. But she's been trying to get everyone to slow down, and she's abstained."

The cop looked me in the eye.

I held her gaze. "Okay, look there are spots for camping about two miles further up. Have you been drinking?"

"I had a beer about an hour ago," I lied.

"Okay, you guys can go, if you promise to go straight to the camp spot, and if you drive."

"You want me to drive?"

"I don't care if she hasn't been drinking, she's clearly in no state to be behind the wheel."

"No problem, Officer. I got this." I walked back to the driver's seat and told Catherine to push over. "Sorry, cop said I gotta drive."

Catherine looked back at the cop who nodded to the affirmative. I got behind the wheel and gave the cop a wave. She drove off.

I slowly backed the car up, and started on my way to the camp spot the cop had recommended.

"Why are you driving so slowly?" Catherine asked.

"I am very drunk, and I do not have a driver's license," I answered.

"Then why did she tell you to drive instead of me?" she whined.

"Because I'm *smooooth*."

I know, drunk driving is no laughing matter, but I can say in my defense that I slowly drove a couple of miles, at night with no other traffic around, under the specific direction of an officer of the law.

Mari changed her mind about buying Catherine's car.

PRIVILEGE

Corona, California, a punk rock show in a storage unit. There were skinheads, Suicidals, and long-haired Mexican guys whom I was told were skinheads, which made no sense at all. It was a fantastic show. In the mosh pit I bumped into someone, which I thought was the whole idea, he started swinging on me. My brother Erick jumped in and started punching back. Lots more punching started happening all around me. A gun came out. The punching stopped.

A tense standoff between two opposing sides was broken by the arrival of many police cars. The surreal no fun disco effect of many sets of red and blue spinning lights all going off non-synchronously made the chaos of the evening even more pronounced. Punks and skinheads were running every which way. Two of my brothers were hurrying me to our car to make our getaway.

We passed a cop and I said, "Excuse, me officer, would you like to suck my dick?"

"What did you say?" he asked.

My brother James answered, "Sorry officer. I'm gonna get him home and beat the shit out of him, I promise."

The cop went back to looking for Mexicans to arrest.

PUBLIC SERVICE ANNOUNCEMENTS

When you're high, don't go to Denny's. I know, it might be the only thing open, they have snacks, but you know who hangs out at Denny's late at night? The cops. And also, the waitress is on harder shit than you and she's bitter and mean and will harsh your vibe big time (Now you have to picture the yellow star going across the screen with the words *"The More You Know"* trailing behind).

All the "Don't Do Drugs" and "Just Say No" PSAs are from people who were bad at doing drugs. What about some positive drug role models? I did drugs, enjoyed them, and stopped doing them before they became a big problem. Let me do a PSA! I'd give good advice like, stay away from white drugs, but if you're gonna do 'em don't do 'em with people you don't know well. The harder the drug, the better you should know your co-pilots.

What I mean to say is, it's cool to smoke pot in the parking lot after the laser show with some folks you just met but if you're gonna drop acid with someone, or go on a coke binge, get references, run a background check, find out their credit score (you don't want it too low, but more importantly, you don't want it too high. Rich dudes will always throw you under the bus if things go sideways).

The More You Know…

"Are you a cop? If you're a cop you have to tell me," is not true. No, for real, it's not. I'm not saying that because I'm a cop. I'm not, trust me. If I was a cop I'd have to tell you.

The More You Know…

My uncle who was a cop advised me, always hit the brakes if you see a cop when you're speeding. I've had people advise me to just slowly let my speed go down, so as not to make them think you have something to hide or some dumb bullshit, but Uncle Andy says "No. Hit the brakes. These guys like power, that's why they're cops. They want you to show them you respect their authority."

The More You Know…

Cops don't like jokes.

The More You Know…

If you do succeed in making a cop laugh and you get out of trouble, this is the equivalent of winning a gold medal in comedy.

The More You Know…

If your boss pays you back for gas receipts, you pay inside at the counter. You give the cashier $30, or $40 and get a receipt. Then you put half that amount in the car. You go back inside and explain that the tank didn't hold as much as you thought it would and get your change. You turn in the receipt for the full amount.

The More You Know…

It's okay to steal from your employer. They're not paying you what you're worth.

The More You Know…

If you have the means you can hire cops to provide security at your event, in their cop uniforms, with their cop weapons, and their cop cars. If you hire them enough they might give you a special sticker to put on your car, and that sticker might just impress a cop who pulls you over, enough that they ask you about it, and then will let you off with a warning even though you made an illegal U-turn during rush hour in San Francisco while driving on a suspended license.

The More You Know...

POT LUCK

Ryan met me in Rocklin, California near my parents' house to exchange Christmas presents. I gave him a UK Subs album on cassette tape. It was an import and not cheap. He gave me a 40oz bottle of Olde English malt liquor that he convinced his brother to buy along with another one for himself.

Ryan was very skinny and suffered from clogged tear ducts which caused his eyes to look puffy and irritated all the time. He had a long mohawk and I frequently told him he looked like a mosquito because he looked like a mosquito. He'd tell anyone who'd listen that he was born prematurely, and it was like some kind of Jedi mind trick.

I watched him receive forgiveness for all kinds of bad behavior because he was born prematurely, and I once saw him get a couple of extra tacos from the nice lady at Taco Bell who a moment earlier was on the verge of banning him for life. As far as I knew, his premature birth had no effect whatsoever on his development and he was just a weird-looking dude with puffy eyes and a penchant for pissing people off.

We lived a constant dilemma being punks in middle-class suburbia. Here we listened and sang along with song after song about anarchy, anticapitalism, and Do It Yourself ethics, but we had few choices but to buy our records and cassettes from the nearest corporate strip mall record store. We'd order directly from the bands who put ads in punk zines, and from the cool indie record stores when we could convince our parents to drive us downtown. My mom had taken me to The Beat twice to get Ryan this UK Subs import, once to special order it, and then again to pick it up when it came in.

"If I liked the UK Subs even a little bit, I'd keep your present, you cheapskate," I told him.

"You're not supposed to give expecting to receive," he replied.

"I figured you'd at least steal me something," I groused.

He and his older brother Jason had a brilliant strategy for stealing from the corporate stores wherein Ryan would flirt with the girl at the cash register, and then casually ask her what the store alarm sounded like. He'd then ask if he could set it off for a laugh. Once he did, his brother and several of his scumbag friends would quickly exit the store, their leather jacks stuffed near to bursting with cassettes and records. Ryan would put back the copy of The Eagles' Greatest Hits or whatever impulse buy cassette was being displayed by the register having used its security tag to set off the alarm. I guess it was too much to think they could cut me in on their booty in honor of our savior's birth.

We found a bridge to drink under as Rocklin had no all-ages hang-out spots other than a gas station/Quickie Mart that was where the metalheads held court. We had a nice buzz on as we finished our bottles, abandoned our position as bridge trolls, and headed toward my folks' place. I'd forgiven Ryan for the shit gift.

We passed a trailer park. Despite all the hacky jokes, not all trailer parks are trash. A lot of them are quite nice, and often they're geared toward retired folks looking for a place without a lot of upkeep but a decent amount of independence. This was one of those. Not a tornado in sight.

I saw a set of carved wooden signs outside their community center and one of them read "Pot Luck," not Potluck but Pot Luck.

I poked Ryan with my elbow, and pointed, "Pot Luck. Ha. That's what kind of luck Billy Has."

We both had a laugh. Billy was the biggest stoner we knew and he was always in trouble with school, parents, and various girlfriends, but he usually skated through, which is to say he wasn't grounded too often and he regularly had sex, and to us that made him about the luckiest bastard we knew.

"We should grab that for him," Ryan suggested.

And so I tiptoed up to the sign and grabbed it. There was no security around and most of the residents had probably long since turned in for the night.

As we continued on toward home I took my jacket off and wrapped it around the sign, so as not to look conspicuous walking down the street carrying it. The cop that turned on his red and blue lights informed us he did so because it looked suspicious, me not wearing my jacket on such a cold night.

We showed him the sign and told him we'd found it and thought it was funny.

"So, I can drive up and down this street and I'm not gonna find a porch missing their sign?" he asked.

"Well, you might. Like I said, we just found it. It must've come from somewhere," I answered. "You want it?"

"I smell alcohol. Have you boys been drinking."

Ryan threw his arms up forming an "X."

"NO SIR!" he yelled, like a cadet in basic training. "I'M STRAIGHT EDGE!"

"You're what now?" the cop asked him.

"STRAIGHT EDGE, SIR! IT'S A YOUTH MOVEMENT OPPOSED TO THE USE AND ABUSE OF DRUGS, ALCOHOL, AND CASUAL SEX, SIR!" Ryan barked.

The cop turned to me.

"Um... yeah, I've had a little bit of beer," I admitted.

"Where'd you get the beer, and don't tell me you found it."

"No. I stole it from my friend's stepdad's fridge. He doesn't know," I answered, figuring this would keep us from getting anyone else in trouble. "I didn't like it so I poured most of it out."

He asked us where we lived, and explained that since we didn't have ID on us, we were technically guilty of vagrancy, and out after curfew, but if my parents were home to confirm we lived where we said we lived, he'd let us off with a warning.

He put us in the back of his squad car. It was my first time in a cop car, and I was nervous but it was also kind of exciting. He parked the black and white car in front of my parent's house, which is something every parent loves. He opened the door to let us climb out for all the gossiping neighbors to see.

He insisted we couldn't just walk in the house. He rang the doorbell and my mom opened the door to see her son and his friend standing with a police officer.

"Evening, Maamme. Do these boys live here?" he asked.

"One of them does," my mom said, glaring hard at me. "And the other one. Is he in your care as well this evening?"

I had not asked my mom about Ryan staying the night but, mad as she was, she was still a pretty cool mom and didn't want to get Ryan in more trouble than we were already in.

"Yes. He's staying the night," she answered.

The cop explained all about the sign, and the beer.

"Are they drunk?" my mom asked.

"Negative, maamme. I'd wager not more than a drop of liquor has touched these boys' tonsils this evening," he said, sounding almost as weird as Ryan had when he'd given his ridiculous "Straight Edge" speech.

We were sloshed. I couldn't decide if the cop had been fooled or if it was a typical case of seeing two young men who looked like him, who came from a decent-looking home, and so a bit of "Boys will be boys" had kicked in. I wasn't in a position to question it.

"Can we keep the sign? I mean, if no one claims it?" Ryan asked, and I had to struggle not to burst out laughing.

"No. You cannot. Have a good night," and with that he was out the door.

As soon as it closed we started laughing. It couldn't be helped.

"Oh, this is funny is it?" my mom asked. "You were drinking?"

"No, mom. You heard him. Not a drop of liquor has touched our tonsils."

"That isn't what he said. Go to bed," she said, not sounding nearly as angry as I thought she'd be.

We went to my room and listened to the UK Subs. They actually weren't too bad and it was a merry Christmas for all.

THE SHINING

It was my first night in my new apartment and I had managed to lock myself out. I had friends with me, and we'd been to the corner store that didn't card us for alcohol purchases. We had all the makings for a party except for a warm place in which to party. My roommate was inside sleeping but no amount of knocking woke him.

I have four brothers. I was constantly locked out of various rooms and houses. As a result, I'm great at breaking in. Friends call me to come to break into their homes for them and I love the challenge almost as much as I love letting them wonder why I'm so good at this.

I found a window lock that would be easy to bounce out of place, and we were in. We got inside and had just cracked open our beers when the cops showed up.

I answered the door to my apartment full of underage drinkers. "Can I help you officers?"

"Yeah, we got a call that some kids were breaking into a vacant apartment," one cop answered.

"Oh, not vacant. I just took over the lease. I had to break in because I locked my keys inside," I explained.

"It looks pretty vacant," he observed, peeking in.

"Like I said, I just moved in. I'll move my furniture over tomorrow."

"Do you have a rental agreement or anything with your name and this address on it?"

"Um… now. Like I said, I just moved in. That stuff is all at my old apartment."

"It seems we have a problem then. We need to know that you're supposed to be here."

They hadn't yet asked about the booze and us being under 21. I was nervous. Then it hit me. "Hey, my roommate is upstairs sleeping. He can vouch for me living here."

"Fine. Let's go talk to him," the cop said to my great relief as he pulled out his flashlight and followed me up the dark stairway.

I opened Chris' door gently. The cop pushed it open wide, and focused his light on my African American roommate's annoyed blinking face.

"Get that fucking light out of my goddamn face now!" Chris yelled, blinded to the fact that he was being awoken by a cop.

I started to question the wisdom of bringing the cop upstairs to Chris.

"Sorry, sir. Does this man live here?" the cop asked, surprisingly polite as he took the light off of Chris and shined it on me.

"Not if he doesn't get the hell out of my room and let me sleep, he doesn't," Chris answered, still not quite clear on what was happening.

The cop apologized again, shut the door, and bid us all a goodnight. Chris was quick to forgive after bumming a cigarette from me. I made a note to put a light in the stairwell.

EL FLACO LOCO VS THE
SACRAMENTO PD

The Colonial Theater on Stockton Blvd opened in 1940, showing Alan Marshall in "Married and in Love" and Lupe Valez in "Mexican Spitfire." In 1999 I made a deal with the theater's owner to screen vintage trash, exploitation, and low-budget horror flicks on Tuesday nights. The theater was dark the rest of the week except on Saturday when they'd show Bollywood films.

The Tuesday Night Grindhouse was born. My partners in this endeavor ran Cinemania, a local video store specializing in grindhouse cinema, B movies, nudie cuties, blacksploitation films, Italian horror, women in prison movies, you know, the good stuff.

Our advertising budget was just enough to print some flyers and press releases at the local Kinkos, and by buying the underage kid there a backpack full of beer from the liquor store down the block I'd get a few extra flyers and maybe some posters. The plan was to be the show that everyone was talking about and this would be achieved not only by having the most outrageous and awesome films, but by staging intermission shows that would make directors like Russ Meyer, Ray Dennis Steckler, and Doris Wishman proud. We used real guns firing blanks after fitting the victim with exploding blood squibs which were wired to the battery of a pickup truck parked outside the emergency exit. A woman rode her motorcycle through the theater during our screening of She-Devils On Wheels. We had "Live Blood Wrestling" (patent pending) while local punk band The Secretions played on the tiny stage, we did it all. RJ, half of the couple that ran Cinemania, ran through the theater with a live chain saw during one of our shows. I asked him afterward how he finally managed to get the chain off.

"Oh, I wasn't able to," he answered, revealing that he'd run around the theater in the dark with a live, fully functioning chainsaw.

For once I was glad our crowds weren't too big. To thank the volunteers who helped us pull together these amazing shows with no budget, we turned the crying room upstairs into a VIP lounge. The crying room had a window that looked out over the audience and the screen, and two speakers carrying in the sound from the movie. It was intended for mothers with crying infants to be able to enjoy a movie without annoying men. We used it to let our volunteers get good and drunk with each other and feel like they were part of something, which of course they were.

Every Tuesday night, as we got more and more extreme in our antics I worried that Mr. Santillian, the owner of the theater, would show up, blow a gasket, and throw us all out. But we took the chance, and we mostly followed his one rule of no porn. Harry Novak randomly cut porn into his print of the 1975 flick Wham Bam Thank You Spaceman to "Spice it up for the 90s" and we pulled an all-nighter cutting it back out before the screening. Barbed Wire Dolls, the 1975 Swiss women in prison movie, turned out to be a bit more graphic than my partners had let on. I was suspicious when they kept not having a copy handy for me to screen in advance. At any rate, Santillian never did show up, and we kept the rent paid on time.

One thing that pushed us to get ever more outrageous was how the local media ignored us. A local film critic listed Spider Baby as one of his favorite movies. We not only played Spider Baby, we brought the director Jack Hill up from LA for the screening. The critic informed us he couldn't make it, had tickets to a play or some such nonsense. I got to watch Spider Baby sitting next to Jack Hill. Any real fan would've been there, I decided. This critic just listed the movie as a favorite because it was cool to say you liked it.

The one local media outlet I did get the attention of was our local FOX affiliate who demanded I stop faxing them pornographic press releases. I called them up.

"Orgy of The Vampires isn't porn. By today's standards, it might not even get an R rating. These are B movies. Stuff Elvira might show," I said honestly thinking I could make a friend, maybe have a laugh over the misunderstanding.

"Your press release has a picture of two naked women chained to a wall."

"What? No! They're in bikinis… um, chained to a wall. It's a horror flick, but it's not porn."

"And what is blood wrestling?"

"Ha! Yeah, that's a parody. It's a parody! You know, like mud wrestling but with fake blood. Look, this stuff is very funny if you can see it through the right lens."

"Mr. Jensen, if you continue to send us this material we will call the police."

"Go ask your film critic! They'll know these movies. This is just a misunderstanding."

"Do not call here again and stop sending us press releases."

I continued sending press releases. They never made good on their promise to call the police on us, sadly.

I heard rumors about a local guy who'd paint pictures with his own blood. Supposedly he'd prick his fingers with needles and apply blood to canvas, going until he passed out. I tracked him down and booked him to perform this feat before the movie. After I'd promoted that he'd be appearing, he backed out. Seems he was a serious artist, and the nature of our show made him feel like it was exploitative.

I assured him that Fulci's Zombie was a cinematic masterpiece that he should be honored to be associated with, but he backed out nonetheless. I'd promised my audience this crazy bloody act. I had to find something that equaled it. I heard of another guy, a dude named Scott who'd drive a nail through his dick. I tracked him down and booked him. He too backed out. I couldn't really argue with someone declining to drive a nail through their penis.

I went to El Flaco Loco, a local luchador (masked Mexican wrestler), and a regular on our stage, to see if he had any ideas. "Keith, just let me put a fake dick down my tights, I'll whip it out, drive a nail through it, and we'll spray more blood through it and onto the audience than ever before."

This meant a lot of blood. I loved this plan. I don't think Mr. Santillian would be thrilled at live bloody dick piercing but it wasn't technically porn.

We offered $1 off admission to anyone wearing a costume and we had one of our best turnouts ever. I heard rumors that members of the band Rancid had driven in for the chance to see Zombie on the big screen. I was having a great time. My friend Michael came as a suicide victim, gun in his hand, little hole on one side of his head, big hole on the other side. I congratulated him on the worst and best costume of the evening.

We got everyone seated, started the movie, and I was headed toward the crying room when my wife grabbed a hold of me. "Keith, there are cops out front with their guns drawn."

I laughed. She didn't. I was baffled at how this could be true. I walked to the front door and looked through the little round window. There were at least a dozen cops in a semi-circle with guns pointed in my direction.

One of them yelled "Come out with your hands where we can see them. Now!"

With my hands up I walked slowly through the door and into their bright lights.

"Get on your knees. Now put your hands behind your head."

I'm on my knees in front of the theater with a dozen guns pointed at me. I look at the cops. Many of them are younger than me. A few have shaky hands. It occurs to me that a car backfiring, or one of my drunk volunteers running out of the theater unaware, and I'm dead. This is not a position I want to remain in.

"Hello," I shouted. "I am the manager of this theater, and I am going to fully cooperate with you. We have a full theater and when intermission hits, they will be coming through that door to smoke. I'd really like it if we could get this resolved before then."

"We received a call that someone was seen entering the theater with a gun."

"That was a cast member!" I shouted, figuring this was much easier than explaining that I gave a dude a dollar off admission for dressing like a suicide victim. "The gun was fake."

"Someone wearing a mask looked out at us, and didn't come out when instructed."

I had to think quickly. It must have been El Flaco. How do I explain that he couldn't come out because the fake rubber penis in his tights was connected to an aquarium pump sitting in a bucket full of fake blood and plugged into the nearest electrical outlet?

"He's a luchador, a masked Mexican wrestler. He couldn't come out because he's... well he's wired to some special effects. But I'm sure he'll come out now."

I called for El Flaco to come out with his hands out where they could see them. He did, and the cops were rough with him. They tackled him to the ground, tore his mask off, and handcuffed him.

"Look, he didn't mean any harm. He was following my instructions. This may seem a silly request, but can we please get his mask back on before the crowd comes out? It's bad for a luchador to be seen without their mask."

I was right. It seemed like a silly request. One that was turned down. Flaco never forgot that even with cops and guns all around me I spoke up to respect the mask and years later still refers to this as proof that I am a true friend of Lucha, which is one of the better compliments I've received in my life.

Luckily they finished running the luchador's ID for warrants and took the handcuffs off of him before Intermission hit. El Flaco Loco hurried around the corner to get back into character, and to get the blood-spraying penis back in his tights.

The cops asked me my name and it turns out Keith Jensen was also the name of one of the cops. Small world. I made note of this information and years later tried to claim he was my uncle to get out of a speeding ticket. It didn't work. But on this night, it was an ice breaker and suddenly the cops were friendlier and their adrenaline started to come down to a reasonable level.

There were still cops everywhere when intermission hit but their guns were back in their hostlers and it just made the show seem that much more badass that a SWAT team had responded to it. El Flaco Loco, the most professional performer I have ever worked with bar none, got his act back together on time, somehow kept his nerves under control, and the penis piercing was a thing of absolute beauty. Best of all, I didn't get shot by a dozen cops.

SMOKING WITH THE FUZZ

I had a new album coming, so my comedy brother Johnny Taylor and I did what we traditionally do when either of us had something new coming out; we smoked cigars and watched the iTunes charts, hopefully, to see some positive movement of an upward trajectory.

I picked Johnny up and we headed for Tobacco Road, my favorite cigar bar. There was a time when I wouldn't have bet on ever having a favorite cigar bar. I average a cigar or two a year only, and usually in my own backyard or around a campfire. But my friend Michael booked comedy shows at Tobacco Road and after performing there a couple of times I found I enjoyed hanging out. The crowd struck me as fairly conservative but they laughed at my jokes when I was on stage and we didn't talk politics otherwise.

My hilarious album sadly came out on the day of the Ferguson riots. A grand jury failed to indict white Police Officer Darren Wilson for shooting Michael Brown, an unarmed black man, to death. This city was engulfed in protests, police overreaction, and riots. Sitting with a good friend and having a cigar while watching both the iTunes charts and the news sounded like decent therapy on this heart-breaking night.

Unfortunately, the other smokers were in less somber of

a mood. A news station played on the large television and jokes were cracked, the atmosphere decidedly jovial. One man, a big boy whom I'd guess was in his thirties, was pacing the floor and commenting on what he'd do if he was there in Ferguson. I considered asking if we could change the subject. I didn't. Johnny and I tried to focus on our own conversation but this proved increasingly difficult.

Then I heard Big Boy say "It's time to call out the National Guard and just have 'em arrest every one of them. Declare a curfew and arrest anyone on the streets, every night, until this shit stops."

Maybe it was the word "them," or how casual this libertarian-leaning, loud fan of freedom was about calling for de facto martial law when it was a black community being discussed, when it was *them*. Something clicked a switch in me and I could control my mouth no more.

"I have a more practical solution. How about cops just stop killing black people?" As the words came out of me, I was aware of two things, the quiet in the room as all eyes turned wide to me, and my friend Johnny, a former Golden Gloves boxer, balling his hands into fists.

Big Boy looked at me dumbfounded. "What did you just say?"

"I said that maybe it'd be simpler for cops to just stop shooting black people all the goddamn time."

I looked around the room and I didn't see spectators watching two people have an argument; I saw hate. I no longer had fans in this room no matter how funny my joke about my nephew struggling to put a condom on a banana had been. Big Boy continued to serve as their spokesperson. I won't bother trying to recollect or paraphrase the garbage he spewed but all the classic racist canards were there, they were destroying their own community, it was just an excuse to rob and steal, and of course that old standby *reverse racism* reared its stupid head.

Occasionally one of the other angry smokers would chime in. One man needed to let me know that he had *black grandchildren, goddamnit* because we all know that if your son or daughter procreates with someone of a different race you yourself cannot possibly be a racist. I kept myself from pointing out that Thomas Jefferson had black grandchildren too, whom he owned. I avoided replying that Strom Thurmond, the segregationist Senator from North Carolina, turned out to have a black daughter as well.

Another man told me I was out of place talking about privilege as I looked like I led a pretty comfortable existence with my sweaters and my nice slacks. I laughed at this, as my clothes come from thrift stores, except for my "nice slacks' which are polyester Wranglers ordered directly from their website. But rather than explain this, I agreed with him because of course he was right about me being privileged. I wasn't calling them privileged as an insult, I was asking them to be aware of our privilege, all of us, myself included. He sarcastically complimented my new sneakers.

Big Boy had gotten worked up enough that his racism was growing more blatant. I started to explain why what he was saying was racist and I was getting worked up enough that whatever tiny shred of diplomacy I'd started with was gone and I may have referenced him talking big while his fat ass was lounging in a cozy cigar bar on the other side of the country having no goddamn idea what the fuck he was talking about.

Big Boy didn't like this. Some four-eyed, sweater-wearing liberal comedian here on his turf calling him out and using the R-word. We white people just can't stand being called Racist, or having our actions described as Racist, or being portrayed as anything other than a wonderful person without a racist bone in our body, who always celebrates Martin Luther King Jr Day, and did we mention we have a black friend (or grandchild)? I'd really done it wielding the R-word, and Big Boy was livid.

"Boy, you're about to get an ass-whooping!" he yelled, his hands tightening into fists.

My survival instincts had either fled or they all went to

mouth hoping to score a knockout with a sharply worded retort. I found myself jumping to my feet and yelling, "Really? Really? You're gonna kick my ass? Really?"

He stopped, confused, waiting to see where this was going before making good on his threat. "That's all it takes to get you to resort to violence? Some skinny twerp smart mouths you at a cigar bar and you're ready to get violent, but you can't understand the violence you're seeing on the screen when they're being shot to death in the street?"

Something amazing and unexpected happened then.

Big Boy blinked, and stared at me for a moment more, and then said. "That's a good point. You just saved yourself from an ass beating."

"Thank you!" I blurted back.

The next day I told Michael, the comedian whose shows had first brought me out to Tobacco Road, about the brouhaha.

He replied, "Yeah, I was worried when I saw you post on Facebook that you and Johnny were heading to a cop hangout last night."

"A cop hangout?"

Michael laughed. "Yeah, you never noticed that most of the guys who hang out there are cops?"

Turns out my comedy album did pretty well over the next week after a slow start that night. I no longer have a favorite cigar bar.

A NOTE FROM THE AUTHOR

I've written these stories of criming while white as I shelter in place, hiding from the COVID-19 pandemic. At first, I'll admit, it was kind of nice having my nights free to explore an old love, playing video games. And when I got that itch to tell a story, I'd pull out my laptop and think about cops, handcuffs, and trying to sleep on hard metal benches. Most of my friends were watching Tiger King and baking sourdough bread. I was taming Divine Beasts in Hyrule, getting tweaked on Skooma in Skyrim, and writing arrest stories.

Later that spring George Floyd and Breonna Taylor were murdered by police and the country exploded into protests, riots, yet more police violence, and lots of tough talk by a man I still can't believe was our president.

I posted on Twitter, "Always remember, they didn't make arrests because they saw the tape; they made arrests because we saw the tape."

My tweet went viral. I was proud to have gotten the words right, but felt odd at having my name thrown into a conversation where my name wasn't important.

I continued working on my stories about cops and arrests. On one hand, it felt good to be writing a collection of stories about the ongoing brutality and idiocy of American police, but on the other hand, it felt odd to be telling mostly funny stories of the many times I got away with "criming while white" when I'd very likely be a felon, in prison, or dead if not for the color of my skin and the privilege it affords me.

But that is the story that I have to tell. I am glad to also have this bit of space to say that I've witnessed firsthand time and time again the racism rampant in our law enforcement and judicial systems.

There was the time my friend Julian and I bought the same bike from the same shop. We were both in our late teens, clean-cut because we were working service industry jobs, and both stoked with our new mountain bikes. I ran into Julian a few weeks later and noticed right away the cool black canvas satchel attached to his handlebars.

"That's nice! I should get one of those. You get them from Midtown Cyclery?" I asked.

"Uh, yeah. To carry my paperwork," he answered.

"What paperwork is that?" I asked.

"Keith, how many times have you been asked to prove you own your bike since you bought it?"

"What? Um… none. Who's asking you to prove you own your bike?"

"The cops, man. Who do you think? They say this model is a high theft item. And I fit the description of a suspect."

Julian was a young black man if that didn't become blatantly obvious by his *fitting the description*.

"The first time it happened I hadn't even made it home from the bike store yet, which is lucky because I still had the receipt on me. So, when they were done with me I rode right back and bought this little bag for the handlebars."

"Damn. I'm sorry," I said, not knowing what else to say.

I felt bad at being surprised by this. And then Julian and I turned our attention to the mayor of Sacramento, our mayor. She was speaking at the state Capital in response to the Rodney King beating and riots in LA and elsewhere after the cops were acquitted even though they'd been caught on video. Our white mayor explained that this kind of racist policing wasn't an issue in Sacramento.

Julian hollered, "No! That's wrong! You're wrong about that!"

And after she offered him some meaningless lip service about wanting to hear from all her citizens, at another time, he rode off on his bicycle with the receipt close at hand.

Of course, this is one of countless examples. Unrest following racist police violence has come to Sacramento in the decades since then, and no doubt will again. In the meanwhile, I continue to ride a bicycle having no idea where the receipt for it even is. Even when the cops impounded my bike to arrest me they gave it back without asking me to prove I owned it. I know I can call the police if my house gets broken into and my car stolen and doing so won't result in me being less safe.

Twenty-some years after my conversation with Julian I was at a comedy show with my friend Hasan Minhaj, a Muslim comedian who was then just starting his ascent to fame.

"You fly a lot, yeah?" he asked me, wanting to know how often I'm pulled aside by the TSA for an extra thorough search.

"Never. Not once."

"And you have a record, right?" he continued.

"I do. In fact, yeah," I answered.

"Amazing. I get pulled aside more often than not. They've actually come on the plane after I've been seated and made me exit to be probed and further harassed."

This struck me as particularly absurd because, whereas Julian and I were pretty similar other than our race, the contrast between me and Hasan couldn't have been sharper. He was the all-American boy, a clean-cut college graduate who took his faith seriously meaning he'd not spent his twenties having the kind of drunken adventures I was known for. Hasan did not have a criminal record. Meanwhile, I'm over here taking the grunge look way past its freshness date, showing up to the airport looking like the disheveled high school dropout with a criminal record that I am, and I skate right through security with my overstuffed backpack every time, so long as I'm not trying to carry a gun into the airport again.

Also striking is the fact that the one time the cops roughed me up, and charged me with felonies was when they thought I was gay.

So yeah, these tales of mouthing off to cops and flouting the law are funny but they're also tales of privilege and I'm sure from some viewpoints they're also bound to be frustrating and depressing. I refuse to condemn shoplifting by people struggling to get enough to eat and to keep sheltered while other people have yachts parked inside their yachts and elevators for their cars, but don't get me wrong; I shoplifted because I was bored and depressed as a teenager. It's not the same thing. I'm glad I got caught and found a new hobby before I got into real trouble, the kind of trouble a black woman shoplifting baby formula and diapers gets into.

To fix the problem with our police is a complicated matter. A gun and a badge are naturally going to attract the wrong kind of person. I'm sure there are good people who want to become cops for noble reasons but can anyone deny that bullies and petty tyrants are going to be drawn to these most accessible trappings of power? Add to this that the white supremacist movement has intentionally sought to infiltrate the ranks of law enforcement for more than a century.*

I hope you've joined or will join the growing movement calling for the problem with American policing to finally be addressed. Make sure you know what defunding the police actually means, and consider that we're putting all our eggs in one basket now. Cops can only respond after a crime has happened. There is a lot we can and should be doing to reduce crime, mostly reducing poverty, confronting institutional racism and income inequity, and addressing drug addiction in a compassionate way centered around education and rehabilitation.

Thanks for reading. Try not to call the cops on each other.

* IN AUGUST OF 2020, Michael German, a former FBI special agent who has written extensively on the ways that US law enforcement have failed to respond to far-right domestic terror threats, filed a report with The Brennan Center for Justice in which he details that US law enforcement officials have been tied to racist militant activities in more than a dozen states since 2000, and hundreds of police officers have been caught posting racist and bigoted social media content.

ACKNOWLEDGMENTS

My wife Bryna, and my daughter Max for their patience when I'd get lost in the words and disappear for hours, for bringing me snacks, and for keeping me around despite my odd penchant for getting arrested.

Greg Proops for telling me, back before my first book, that I was smart enough to write a book, and for the most Proopsian of intros to this book.

Aaron Carnes and Amy Bee for encouragement, editorial help, and making me feel like I must be a somewhat decent writer to have two such amazing writers willing to give me their time.

CLASH Books, for letting me tell my story my way and for being the coolest publishers around.

Kirk Larsen, Chris Kortright, KX Emm, Coal Bottel Dorius, and Chris Brunner for being there for me when I got my face kicked and threatened with a felony.

Johnny Taylor for being down to fight cops with me.

Carrie Poppy, thanks again for getting me my first book deal. I owe you mango and sticky rice

Thanks to Mom and Dad for being surprisingly understanding about all of this.

Thank you to every cop who has ever crossed that blue line, risking your career and safety to stand up for what's right.

ABOUT THE AUTHOR

Keith Lowell Jensen has performed for over 20 years as a stand up comedian, delighting crowds from New York to Shanghai. He's a guest lecturer at The University of California, Davis. He boasts 8 comedy specials to his credit which have earned him accolades from the Wall Street Journal, Time Out NY, and a guest spot on The History Channel's *How The States Got Their Shapes*.

What I Was Arrested For is Jensen's second book, following 2018's *Punching Nazis and Other Good Ideas*.

When not stand-up comedying or sitting down writing, Jensen can be found drinking really good coffee and hanging out with his wife, Bryna, their daughter Max, and their cat Marmalade, in Sacramento, California.

ALSO BY CLASH BOOKS

BORN TO BE PUBLIC

Greg Mania

LIFE OF THE PARTY

Tea Hacic

PROXIMITY

Sam Heaps

DARRYL

Jackie Ess

GAG REFLEX

Elle Nash

HEXIS

Charlene Elsby

MARGINALIA

Juno Morrow

I MADE AN ACCIDENT

Kevin Sampsell

HIGH SCHOOL ROMANCE

Marston Hefner

ILL BEHAVIOR

M. Stevens S.

WE PUT THE LIT IN LITERARY

clashbooks.com

FOLLOW US

Twitter

IG

FB

@clashbooks

CPSIA information can be obtained
at www.ICGtesting.com
Printed in the USA
JSHW020815041122
32487JS00006B/6